A CENTURY OF
SOCIAL CATHOLICISM
1820–1920

A CENTURY OF
SOCIAL CATHOLICISM
1820–1920

BY

A. R. VIDLER

LONDON

S·P·C·K

First published in 1964
Paperback edition 1969
by S.P.C.K.
Holy Trinity Church
Marylebone Road
London N.W.1

Made and printed in Great Britain by
William Clowes and Sons, Limited
London and Beccles

SBN 281 02436 7

Contents

Preface

This book is based on the course of lectures which the Scott Holland Trustees kindly invited me to deliver at King's College, London, in February 1960. Various circumstances prevented me from preparing them for publication at once. They now appear in an expanded form, but they are designed to be no more than an introduction for English readers to a subject that is not only of importance in itself but of a lively interest because of contemporary developments in Roman Catholicism in Europe. The words "Catholicism" and "Catholic" are used throughout to mean Roman Catholicism and Roman Catholic without prejudice to the question whether they can be properly applied to other Christians as well.   A. R. V.

Introduction

I must begin by explaining what is meant by "social catholicism" since, although this expression has a recognized meaning on the Continent, it is not at all familiar in England and it does not bear its meaning on its face. "Catholicism" of course signifies that what is in question is an aspect of the thought and practice of people who are catholics. But surely catholicism is by definition *social*. No one can be a real catholic without belonging to a society, namely the Church. Is it not then a pleonasm to attach to the substantive "catholicism" the epithet "social"?

The expression "social catholicism" was not invented merely to emphasize the fact that catholicism binds people together in a society. It is intended to direct attention to a particular form or aspect of catholicism which is concerned with the welfare of society, that is, of human beings in their social relations. But it is intended to be much more specific than that, for it refers to a movement or trend in catholicism that first appeared in the nineteenth century. Catholicism has always been social in the sense that it has had a more or less definitely articulated doctrine about man's social nature and his social obligations—for example, about the family, civil government, the relations of Church and State, and the duty of compassion for the poor—as well as about the purely religious or ecclesiastical duties of members of the Church such as attendance at public worship.

"Social catholicism" presupposes all that, but none of that is its distinguishing mark.

Social catholicism, in the technical sense in which the term is here being used, has to do with the consequences of the Industrial Revolution and the changes that took place in those countries that were industrialized and with the ways in which catholics reacted or responded to those consequences and changes. I shall be describing these reactions and responses in four representative European countries—France, Belgium, Germany, and Italy—and most fully in France where the manifestations of social catholicism were more varied and extensive than elsewhere. But first I will briefly recall the principal social effects of the Industrial Revolution which took place first in England and, as we shall see, later and more gradually in the other countries. Its characteristic effects, however, were similar everywhere, and they included urbanization, pauperism, and a new stratification of classes.

As E. R. Wickham has said, "the Europe that was christianized was a peasant and peasant-artisan society, in which the mass of men lived, worked and died in small communities".[1] Broadly speaking, there were no large cities before the nineteenth century. An inevitable result of industrialization was the bringing into being of heavy concentrations of population. Masses of people were uprooted from the land and from the life of small communities in which each knew all the others, and were herded together in urban conglomerations. One of the many lamentable features of these new concentrations of population was a new kind of poverty.

There has always been poverty in the world, but the Industrial Revolution led to a new kind of poverty which is appropriately called "pauperism". Large sections of society were degraded and deprived of tolerable conditions of livelihood and

[1] "Christian Faith and Modern Technological Society" (Art.), *The Ecumenical Review* (April 1959), p. 259.

of a tolerable life in common with others. While the industrial capitalists were accumulating large fortunes, the conditions of the workers went from bad to worse. "Starvation wages were paid; employment was uncertain; women and children were toiling twelve and fourteen hours a day in the new factories, under unhealthful and often immoral conditions. . . . Drunkenness and disease were undermining the stamina of the race."[1]

Industrialism produced a new class stratification—a more powerful middle class between the old landed aristocracy and those who were subordinate to it, a new *bourgeoisie* that was avid to exploit the new sources of wealth, and above all it produced a proletariat. What had been known (in England) as "the labouring poor" became "the working class". There was no homogeneous relationship between these classes. Their interests were antagonistic to one another. The working class would have to struggle hard if it was to remedy the conditions in which it was forced to live and work.

Another circumstance of great importance was the dominance, in the countries affected, of the doctrine of *laissez faire* which derived from the eighteenth century and was developed by the leading political economists of the nineteenth century. It was supposed to be the function of government to refrain from obstructing the automatic and beneficent operation of economic laws and free competition. There should be no legislative interference with the working of the industrial system.

The expression "social catholicism" designates those individuals and groups in catholicism that became aware of these social changes, that were shocked by their inhumanity, that refused to sit down under the doctrine of *laissez faire*, and that

[1] P. T. Moon, *The Labor Problem and the Social Catholic Movement in France: A study in the History of Social Politics* (New York, 1921), p. 1. This book contains much useful information and many references to the literature that was available when it was published.

determined to do something more to ameliorate the consequences of industrialization than could be done by traditional
charity. The actual expression "social catholicism" did not come
into use till towards the end of the nineteenth century, but
realities come into existence before satisfactory words are discovered to denote them.[1] What is meant by social catholicism
began to become a reality quite early in the century.

Amid all its varied manifestations it represented the belief that
it was possible and a matter of moral obligation to improve the
social structure as well as to bring charitable relief to the victims
of industrialism, although in the early stages it was not always
easy to draw so sharp a distinction. Those who are to be described
as social catholics were not fatalistic, but believed in the possibility of consciously directed change, though the kind of change
desired might be more backward-looking than forward-looking.
That is to say, they might advocate the revival of the corporations
that had been destroyed by the French Revolution (social
catholicism of the right) or the construction of a new social order
along democratic or socialistic lines (social catholicism of the
left). Social catholicism could be either revolutionary or reforming: it might stand either for an attempt to replace the existing
social system by a different one or for the introduction of
ameliorative measures into the existing system by legislation and
by organizing social pressures and social services. Again, social
catholicism could be both theoretical and practical: it could
enunciate doctrine or express itself in distinguishable kinds of
action.

[1] Duroselle (see n. 2 on p. 3), p. 21, points out that the emergence of the expression "social catholicism" was delayed, in France at all events, by the fact
that in the middle of the nineteenth century the word "social" was used in a
purely conservative sense by men who wanted to preserve the fabric of society
from the threat of change and reform. See also A. Dansette, *Religious History of
Modern France* (1961), ii, 112.

PART ONE

I

France before 1848

The effects of industrialization were beginning to appear in France during the period of the Restoration and they gathered momentum throughout the period of the July monarchy, though industrial expansion was more gradual in France than in England and it should be remembered that France was still a predominantly agricultural country even at the beginning of the twentieth century.[1] The earliest manifestations of social catholicism were both practical and theoretical, but they cannot be clearly marked off from the traditional idea that there was a Christian obligation to help the poor.

In 1822 there was founded in Paris a Society of St Joseph to meet some of the needs of industry.[2] It was an offshoot of the Congregation, which was the name of an association that had been started in the time of the Napoleonic Empire in order to fortify catholics, chiefly of the upper classes, in a devout way of life and in works of charity.[3] The Society of St Joseph was founded with the purpose of providing employers with good workers, but it had the correlative aim of training workers and of supplying educational and welfare services for them, especially for the young people who came to Paris from the provinces in

[1] See F.-A. Isambert, *Christianisme et classe ouvrière* (1961), p. 120.

[2] Except where other references are given, I refer for documentation concerning social catholicism in France prior to 1870 to J.-B. Duroselle, *Les Débuts du catholicisme social en France, 1822–1870* (1951)

[3] See G. de Grandmaison, *La Congrégation, 1801–1830* (²1890).

3

search of employment. They were put in touch with respectable lodgings, and provision was made for useful ways of occupying their spare time, wholesome forms of recreation, and opportunities of practising their religion. It was also a friendly society which insured its members against sickness, and in fact it offered to young workers most of the amenities that were offered by the university settlements in London later in the century. It appears to have had branches in several provincial towns to which workers could be commended if they moved from Paris.

The Society of St Joseph had a considerable success and even prestige. It was patronized by the royal family. Lamartine, who was at this time a royalist and a catholic, composed a cantata for it! It began with the support of about 200 employers, and finally had the support of 1,000, and it had about 7,000 workers on its books. (There was also a Society of St Nicholas which provided for the training of apprentices.) The Society of St Joseph was dissolved in 1830 when the Restoration monarchy fell. Like the Congregation, from which it had sprung, it was discredited by its legitimist associations, that is to say, by the attachment of its promoters to the cause of the Bourbon dynasty. That is a factor that bedevilled, or at least complicated, the history of French catholicism throughout the century. The significance of the Society of St Joseph is that it set a pattern for many later social catholic activities and enterprises.

The earliest evidence of theoretical or literary awareness on the part of a French catholic about the problems raised by industrialism is an article that was written by Félicité de Lamennais (1782–1854) about the Society of St Joseph in 1822, the year of the Society's foundation.[1] Lamennais, in this as in other respects, was gifted with prophetic insight into the changes that were taking place in society. At this time he was still a royalist who attributed the ills of society to the disintegrating and demoraliz-

[1] Concerning Lamennais, see my book *Prophecy and Papacy: A study of Lamennais, the Church and the Revolution* (1954).

4

ing effects of the French Revolution. In this article he painted a dark picture of the dechristianized state of France; he recalled how much had been owed in the past to the Christian missionary enterprise; and in particular he extolled the ancient trade guilds that had been under the auspices of the Church. Those closely knit associations, he said, had conferred many benefits on the workers, and their destruction was to be deplored. As it was, he wrote:

> Paris has a vast population which includes a multitude of workers of all sorts. Some are settled in a fixed job; others come from elsewhere to practise their trade temporarily; finally, there are many young people who arrive from the provinces in order to learn a trade or to improve themselves in that which they have already adopted. . . .
>
> It is dreadful to contemplate the condition of so many decent young people who are drawn to Paris each year . . . and who find themselves witnesses of a licentiousness which unhappily is only too contagious. Without any bearings, without supervision or advice; surrounded by seductions; lost, so to speak, in this crowd of vices which press upon them and solicit them from every side; how can they fail to succumb? How can they preserve the religious sentiments, the sound morals, and the simple and regular habits, which most of them bring with them from the provinces? It is practically impossible: experience proves that only too well.[1]

Lamennais therefore called for enthusiastic support for the Society of St Joseph. He realized that the dissolution of the old social order and the new developments in industry had created a new situation which constituted a challenge to catholics. Of this article it has been justly remarked that Lamennais' views "are far in advance of what was then called the spirit of the age and consequently of the outlook of the liberals of the period".[2]

---

[1] See Lamennais, *Œuvres complètes*, viii, 252, 255f. The article appeared in the *Drapeau Blanc*, 20 November 1822.

[2] C. Maréchal, *La Mennais au Drapeau Blanc* (1946), p. 38.

The liberals, with their confidence in the doctrine of *laissez faire*, hardly bothered themselves about the wretched condition of the proletariat.

Six months later Lamennais returned to the subject in an article on Sunday observance. In addition to traditional considerations about its value, the article contains passages such as the following:

> The deep degradation, the loathsome oppression, of the indigent class is a natural and inevitable effect of the materialism that rules in our society. Only religion protects the poor and teaches the rich to respect the poor; and if it did no more than that, the human race would have reason to be grateful for it. Modern politics, on the other hand, absorbed as it is with material interests, which alone it deems to be *positive*,—as if for nations morality were not as real an interest as tariffs, and as if the decalogue were not as *positive* as the budget;—modern politics, I say, sees in the poor only a slot machine from which as much as possible must be extracted in a given time. It estimates its usefulness by what it produces, just as it estimates the usefulness of the rich by what they consume, because the wealth of the State, that is to say, taxation, increases in proportion to production and consumption. . . . What you are going to have is industrial helots, whom for a bit of bread you confine in workshops, and who will live and die without perhaps ever having heard of God, without any knowledge of duty, and often without any family ties, without any desires except those of animals, and without any fear other than that of the hangman.
>
> I know it will be answered: At any rate they are free. In truth, there are strange ideas of what liberty is, and a remarkable value is assigned to this fantastic liberty, when it is thought to be sufficient to compensate for the loss of all that contributes to the dignity and happiness of man. Do not let us deceive ourselves. These unfortunate people are not free. The terrible domination that you exercise over them is proof enough of that. Their needs make them dependent on you; necessity makes them your slaves. . . . [1]

[1] See Lamennais, *Œuvres complètes*, viii, 326f. The article appeared in the *Drapeau Blanc*, 24 May 1823.

It will be seen that Lamennais here attacks the evil effects of industrialism not only on religious or moral, but on social, grounds. The plight of the workers was a result of the faulty organization of society and of the inhuman, utilitarian assumptions of those who controlled it. Here we certainly have an anticipation of social catholicism. Indeed, it suggests one of the "might-have beens" of church history.

Lamennais might have been the founder and inspirer of social catholicism, just as he was the founder of liberal catholicism and the principal influence in converting the French Church from gallicanism to ultramontanism. But it was to those causes, and not to social catholicism, that he was to devote his energies until his rupture with the Church a dozen years later. It was only after his break with catholicism that he finally dedicated himself to the service of the working class and became a socialist; a dedication that was at last fitly symbolized by his being buried in a pauper's grave at his own request. Lamennais' socialism cannot be included in the story of social catholicism since, by the time he really gave himself to it, he had ceased to be a catholic and was treated by the Church as an apostate.

Nevertheless, before the rupture he indirectly played a part in its genesis, for in the periodical the *Avenir* (1830-1) he welcomed with both arms some important contributions on the subject from one of his collaborators, Charles de Coux (1787-1864).[1] De Coux was a layman whose father had emigrated with his family to America in 1790. They did not return to France till 1803. Not very much is known about de Coux (no biographical study of him has ever been written), but he does not appear to have been brought up as a catholic. The teaching of Malthus directed his attention to the population question and to social

[1] On de Coux as a precursor of social catholicism, see Duroselle, pp. 40-57. See also "The nature of the *Avenir* Movement" (art.), *American Historical Review* (July 1960), pp. 837-47, by P. N. Stearns, who considers that there were at least three substantially different attitudes among the contributors, Lamennais, de Coux, and Gerbet being the most progressive.

problems generally, and it was because he came to believe that catholicism pointed the way to a solution of them that he became a catholic. But he had published nothing before 1830, and it was only then that he began to express his ideas.

De Coux had a lively sense of the miserable condition of the industrial workers, and he did not mince his words in advertising, as the source of the evil, the heartless greed of the capitalist class. Thus he wrote in the *Avenir*:

> Who is it that everywhere stands in the way of the political emancipation of the masses? It is the great barons of industrialism, these men who fix wages at their pleasure and who reckon that they have replaced the restraining influence of religious beliefs by the threat of a kind of individual famine that will immediately beset the proletarian who is locked out of their workshops.... Already the industrial system is producing everywhere its most bitter fruits.[1]

This industrialism, which was spreading its evil influence even to agriculture, was repeatedly denounced by de Coux. Property was concentrated in the hands of the few. Stock-farming was taking the place of agriculture and so depriving numerous families of their livelihood. "But what does this matter to the owner? A bullock brings him in more than a man and he prefers the bullock."[2] The relations between owners and workers ceased to be human and if this went on the capitalists would reap what they were sowing, namely a revolt of the working class.

The workers should be free to combine with a view to their getting a better share of the proceeds of their labour. De Coux was a convinced advocate of trade unionism, and in this respect he was in advance of most nineteenth-century social catholics. He also attacked the question of limiting the hours of work. He

[1] Art. in the *Avenir*, 21 April 1831; see *Articles de l'Avenir*, iv, 31.
[2] Art. in the *Avenir*, 25 June 1831; see *Articles de l'Avenir*, v, 129.

saw the solution of the social problem in applying the principles of democracy, which were also the principles of catholicism (a favourite theme of the *Avenir*).

> Give the worker the right to vote and this cold war which is exhausting our commerce will come to an end of itself. The proletarian will always have something to give to the manufacturer in exchange for the benefits that he will receive from him, namely his vote. Not only his labour but his friendship will have to be sought in order to do business. [1]

After the condemnation of the *Avenir*, de Coux continued to write and to lecture on social questions and on political economy, but although he aimed at making his thought more precise and more scientific there was a comparative timidity in his subsequent teaching. It would seem that, in his case as in the case of others who made their submission, the condemnation of the *Avenir* had the effect of damping down a fire that had promised to make a fine blaze.

De Coux was not the only contributor to the *Avenir* who was outspoken in this field. Philippe Gerbet (1798–1864),[2] one of Lamennais' closest disciples and collaborators, prophesied in glowing terms about a new social order which would be governed by intelligence and conscience instead of by brute force, and in which the priest would be a man of the people, sacrificially identifying himself with the interests of all who were in need. Gerbet was very eloquent, but somewhat vague and utopian. A course of lectures in this vein which he delivered in 1832 to students in Paris on "The Philosophy of History" evoked great enthusiasm, not least in Frédéric Ozanam who was also influenced by de Coux and who was to play a notable part in the social catholic movement as the founder of the Society of St Vincent de Paul.[3] Gerbet, who in 1832 looked like becoming a socialist,

---

[1] Art. in the *Avenir*, 6 April 1831; see *Articles de l'Avenir*, iii, 428f.

[2] On Gerbet, see C. de Ladoue, *Mgr Gerbet*, 3 vols. (1872).

[3] See p. 24 below.

moved no further in that direction, and by the time he was made a bishop in 1853 he had retreated from his mennaisian idealism into a conventional conservatism. In fact, he was the author of an early draft of Pio Nono's *Syllabus errorum*.[1]

This is not, however, to say that conservatism in France was necessarily antithetic to social catholicism. On the contrary, just as in England Robert Southey and Benjamin Disraeli and Young England reacted positively and imaginatively to the effects of the Industrial Revolution, so in France there were conservative catholics who contributed to the origins as well as to the development of social catholicism.

One of these was Viscount Alban de Villeneuve-Bargemont (1784–1850).[2] He was of an aristocratic family which had not emigrated during the Revolution. He and his brothers served both Napoleon and the restored Bourbons with distinction in a variety of public offices. Indeed, Louis XVIII is reported to have said that he would like to have had as many Villeneuves as there were departments in France: then he would have made all eighty-six of them prefects!

Alban himself was prefect of several departments in succession, and finally of the department du Nord from 1828 to 1830. After the July Revolution he was retired on a pension. He had always been a man of thought as well as of action—a student of political economy, especially of the physiocrats from whom he had learned to evaluate agriculture above industry. His experience as a prefect in the industrial north confirmed his detestation of the English pattern of industrialism. He had attacked the problem in a long report that he made to the Government in 1829. He said that a vast scheme of amelioration should be undertaken to improve the deplorable and degraded condition of the workers.

[1] See R. Aubert, *Le pontificat de Pie IX* (1952), p. 248.
[2] See Duroselle, pp. 59–71, who says that Villeneuve-Bargemont "est vraiment l'initiateur du catholicisme social dans les milieux conservateurs".

Public order, humanity and justice impose on national and local government the duty first to discover means of relieving the sufferings of this large body of poor people, then to tackle the cause of this wretched state of affairs. . . . The principal question, the chief aim, must be to extinguish the causes which perpetuate destitution so that it will no longer be the hereditary lot of a portion of the population, but only one of the exceptional or accidental hazards of the social order.[1]

Among the remedies which Villeneuve-Bargemont proposed were healthy housing; the restoration of religion and habits of temperance; education, "in order that the worker should not be tied down to being an animated machine capable of only a single function, that went to waste if it was not in use"; and compulsory savings. Beyond that, he looked to a vast transplantation of population by the creation of agricultural colonies.

Villeneuve-Bargemont's enforced leisure after the July Revolution set him free to extend his investigations and to elaborate his ideas, which he did in an enormous *Treatise on Christian Political Economy*. A visit to Lille, where there were almost 32,000 paupers in a population of 70,000, made a tremendous impression on him.[2] He wanted France to work out an industrial system which would be different from that in England with its characteristic pauperism—*le pauperisme anglais*. The Christian religion, he said, is indubitably the only foundation for a social order that is in conformity with the nature of man. It called not only for charity but for an enlightened reordering of the national economy which would not however be egalitarian. The primary need was to produce not more luxuries but sufficient of the necessities of life.

He was opposed to *laissez faire* and favourable to government intervention.

If it is true that, by reason of the more or less greedy pursuit of their interests by speculators, the working class finds itself habitually

[1] Ibid., p. 62.   [2] See Moon, op. cit., p. 20.

without adequate wages, and sometimes even deprived of work, and that, apart from some honourable exceptions, no care is taken of the health or welfare or education or morality of the workers . . . there can be no doubt that the legislature must intervene.[1]

The most efficacious service that government could render would be to establish agricultural colonies on land that was neglected but capable of cultivation, and he maintained that there was plenty of that in France. Villeneuve-Bargemont himself took part in the foundation of more than one such colony. As regards industry, he said that attention should be concentrated on the problems of distribution rather than of production.

I turn now to the early Christian socialists: they constituted another source of French social catholicism, which emerged independently and had scarcely any contact with those that we have so far considered. Socialism, in the sense of projects for reform based on social organization in place of individual competition, received a considerable impetus from the July Revolution. Before that, socialism had been the creed of an esoteric sect, the Saint-Simonians. The failure of the July monarchy, with its vaunted liberalism, to touch the evils of industrialism and pauperism, made men with a social conscience readier to consider radical ideas.

Of the disciples of Saint-Simon (1760–1825) it has been said that

in face of the ruin of the old ideas and the bankruptcy of the new ones,—in face of the destruction of the *ancien régime*, the defeat of the monarchy and the Church, and the embarrassed powerlessness of triumphant liberalism which was incapable of getting beyond criticism and negation,—the disciples of Saint-Simon claimed that they alone had a positive message and were able to provide the prescription for a new society. Turning from the political parties

[1] See Duroselle, p. 67.

which had refused to listen to them, they addressed themselves directly to the proletariat. They called upon the workers to repudiate the vain dreams of liberalism, in order to concentrate on the one thing that ought to interest them: namely, the creation of human institutions which would assure to them the daily bread that they would no longer need to beg from God. They pointed to the exasperating contrast between the mass of the people "who produce everything and possess nothing and the privileged minority which produces nothing and enjoys everything". These, they said, were the two great parties, and the struggle between them ought to take the place of the futile controversies of politics.[1]

The Saint-Simonians themselves were led into the wilderness or up the garden path under the fantastic leadership of Père Enfantin, but other socialists—Pierre Leroux, Philippe Buchez, Charles Fourier, Louis Blanc, Proudhon—were soon emboldened to work out, and claim a hearing for, their ideas. They did not all make a direct contribution to social catholicism, but two of them—Buchez and Fourier—certainly did. Two types of Christian socialism may be said to have derived from their influence. These early Christian socialists were catholics who believed in the dogmas of the Church, even if they did not scruple to criticize the pope and the hierarchy, and at the same time they believed in the need to combine catholicism with socialism. Some of them were socialists who were more or less converted to catholicism, and others were catholics who were more or less converted to socialism.

The central figure in the first group was Philippe Buchez (1796–1865).[2] He came of revolutionary stock. He began his career under Napoleon I as a customs official, but resigned from the government service when the Bourbons returned, and he set himself to qualify as a doctor. In 1820 he was one of the founders

[1] See E. Fleury, *Hippolyte de la Morvonnais: sa vie, ses œuvres, ses idées* (1911), p. 286.

[2] On Buchez, see Armand Cuvillier, *P.-J.-B. Buchez et les origines du socialisme chrétien* (1948); Duroselle, pp. 81–120.

of the French carbonari, a secret society which aimed at advancing radical ideas in politics and religion, and which is said within a year or two to have acquired 80,000 members. Buchez became a Saint-Simonian after the death of Saint-Simon in 1825, but he broke with the party when Père Enfantin turned it into a pantheistic religious cult.

Buchez was thus well furnished with radical and socialistic ideas and impulses before he became a convinced catholic early in the 1830s. Eventually he attained a brief eminence in the eyes of the world when he was the first President of the National Assembly in 1848. When the Second Empire was established, he had to retire from political action, but he remained faithful to his Christian socialist beliefs till his death in 1865.

Of his conversion to Christianity he wrote in retrospect:

> I was convinced that I should find in Christianity all that I had long desired, and I regretted that those who had taught me in my youth and the *philosophes* had sent me so far off the track in search of the truth when I had it so close to me. I studied Christianity; I learned its history; I found there the origins of everything I admired and respected; I read there why France was the eldest daughter of the Church; I found there not only the proof but the precise indication of the most fruitful scientific ideas and, among others, of the doctrine of progress which explains so many things; I admired and I believed as I did when I was a little child.[1]

He became a Christian because he found in Christianity a faith that promised to realize the equality and brotherhood of men and deliver them from the egoism that sets them one against another and class against class. It was to the catholic form of Christianity that Buchez was attracted, and to which he attached himself, on account of its social implications, but he never became a practising member of the Church.

He did not want to drive a wedge between himself and his

[1] See Duroselle, pp. 82f.

republican associates. He wanted to serve as an intermediary between republicanism and catholicism, and his influence as an intermediary was one of the factors that made the 1848 Revolution, unlike that of 1830, friendly to the Church.[1] But Buchez's decision to stop short of becoming a practising catholic had another cause. He was very critical of some aspects of ecclesiastical discipline and piety, and he was determined to be free to speak his mind. For example, he said that the encyclical *Mirari vos* issued in 1832 by Gregory XVI—the encyclical by which the *Avenir* was condemned—was the utterance of a "perjured" pope who had "let himself be tied to the back of the chariot of civilization in order to retard its progress".

> One looks in vain for a Christian thought in this bragging and platitudinous Italian chatter, which can do no more than repeat the everlasting harangues of the reactionaries on liberty, the press, and revolutions. . . . There is not a kind word in it, not a word of pity for those who suffer; all its solicitude is for the princes and the potentates, as though Jesus Christ had been executed in order to justify the power of the Patricians who condemned him.[2]

That was only too true, but it was not language that would have been tolerated in a practising catholic.

The social teaching of Buchez proceeded from an analysis of the evils of competition and the class struggle. "European society to-day", he said, "is divided into two classes . . . one is in possession of all the instruments of labour: land, factories, houses, capital; the other has nothing, it works for the former. . . ."[3] The workers were completely in the hands of the employers as regards both their rate of wages and the obligations that were

[1] "La différence qui existe, sous le rapport de la tolérance religieuse, entre la Révolution de Juillet et celle de 1848, vient en grande partie de l'influence qu'eut l'école de Buchez sur le parti du *National*." E. Cartier, *Vie du Révérend Père Besson*, quoted by Cuvillier, op. cit., p. 60.

[2] See Duroselle, p. 83.

[3] See Cuvillier, op. cit., p. 38.

imposed on them. They were not allowed to combine in order to defend themselves. For such a state of affairs Christian charity and philanthropy were not more than feeble palliatives.

The only remedy lay in a new social order based on co-operation. In particular, Buchez advocated the formation of democratic, profit-sharing co-operative societies of producers, by means of which the workers could gradually acquire and control capital and become their own employers. He had a scheme by which credit could be made available to them. "It was by co-operation", he said, "that the industrial classes five centuries ago threw off feudal slavery; it is by co-operation that the wage-earners of our time will throw off the equally grinding slavery to which they are subjected by the capitalists."[1]

Buchez was a vigorous and persistent propagandist. By lecturing and writing, and by his own dedication to the socialist cause, he gathered a large and varied body of adherents, with whose help he founded periodicals and proclaimed a revolutionary catholicism. "This great social crisis", he declared, "cannot be solved till the day when the revolutionaries are catholics and the catholics are revolutionaries."[2] His collaborators and supporters included doctors, artists, soldiers, men of letters (Alfred de Vigny at one time regarded himself as a member of the school), as well as men who were actually engaged in industry. Some of Buchez's most devoted disciples became Dominicans when his friend Lacordaire restored the Order of Preachers in France.

The buchezians were socialists, not communists. They were opposed to violence. One of the ablest of them, however, a lawyer by profession, wrote sympathetically of the communists.

Communism is in reality only the great protest of labour against the domination of capital. No doubt this protest is badly formulated and proposes a remedy worse than the disease . . . but it attacks a real evil, it is provoked by an open sore that requires drastic treat-

[1] See Duroselle, p. 93. [2] See ibid., p. 97.

ment. . . . It is not enough to reject the communist system, and to prove that it is absurd; it is also necessary, if its advance is to be arrested, to propound and apply good remedies instead of bad ones.[1]

Buchez came near to enrolling the Archbishop of Paris, Mgr Affre, among his collaborators. Denis-Auguste Affre (1793–1848)[2] was a prelate of independent outlook who had long been concerned about social problems. In the summer of 1847 both he and Buchez were staying for some weeks at Cauterets in the Pyrenees. They became acquainted and saw much of each other and seem to have discovered that they had much in common. It may be that the welcome accorded by the archbishop to the Second Republic in the following year was partly the result of his contact with Buchez. Unfortunately, his death on the barricades in June 1848 prevented their friendship from developing further.

Perhaps the most interesting group that regarded Buchez as its master was composed of the working men who published a journal called the *Atelier* from 1840 to 1850.[3] These men were in varying degrees catholic. Some regarded Christianity as supplying the moral sanction for their socialist faith, some abandoned the Church, but others were fully catholic, and one of the most striking, C.-F. Chevé (b. 1813), owed his conversion to Buchez. He said that Buchez "was for a large number of young people who had imbibed democratic ideas the providential instrument and means of their conversion to catholicism".[4]

The *Atelier* went further than Buchez in its assaults on capitalism, and it wanted to revive the Church's condemnation of usury. While it espoused the cause of co-operation, it stood for the formation of a national structure of co-operative societies,

[1] Auguste Ott: see Duroselle, p. 108.

[2] On Affre, see P. Poupard, *Correspondance inédite entre Mgr A. Garibaldi internonce à Paris et Mgr C. Mathieu archevêque de Besançon* (1961), pp. 78–95.

[3] See Cuvillier, *Un Journal d'Ouvriers, "L'Atelier"* (1914).

[4] See Duroselle, p. 115.

an organized co-operative state, instead of leaving the formation of co-operative societies to sporadic local initiative. The
members of this group were also more virulent in their attacks
on attempts to meet the condition of the proletariat with mere
charity or organized almsgiving. For example, in an article
directed against the Society of St Vincent de Paul[1] we read:

> It was not with alms that the slavery of antiquity was brought to an
> end; it was not with alms that the serfdom of the middle ages was
> brought to an end; and it will not be with alms that the wage-
> earners of industrial serfdom will be liberated. And this is why we
> denounce organized almsgiving of which the well-known and
> almost avowed object is to make the workers put up with their
> inferior status for as long as possible.[2]

And again:

> What the people demand is not alms, nor patronage whether
> philanthropic or religious; it is not even bread they ask for, if
> attached to it there are conditions of slavery. What they want is
> their place in the home of the great family and the recognition of
> their right to take part in public affairs. What they want is freedom
> to reap what they sow by their labour; the abolition of all financial
> privilege. . . . No one desires more than we do that the clergy
> should intervene in the questions about emancipation which the
> masses of the people are to-day raising; but this intervention must
> be informed by a truly Christian spirit.[3]

M. Duroselle, who is the chief authority on the history of
social catholicism in this period, concludes that "the *Atelier*
represents, on the frontiers of social catholicism, the only attempt
of which we know to create a workers' movement under
Christian inspiration".[4]

The other socialist theoretician who directly influenced a considerable number of catholics, though he did so for the most part

---

[1] On the Society of St Vincent de Paul, see pp. 24f. below.
[2] See Duroselle, p. 118.   [3] See ibid., pp. 119f.   [4] Ibid.

posthumously, was Fourier. Charles Fourier (1772–1837)[1] had published his social theories before 1830, but it was not till after that date that he really won a hearing. He was not himself a Christian, but his teaching or parts of it could at least be represented as compatible or congruent with Christianity. While he agreed with Buchez in denouncing individualism and competition and in wanting to establish the principle of co-operation, his system had peculiar features.

Its key-word was "harmony", and it involved a metaphysical and a psychological, as well as an economic, doctrine. The principle of harmony, according to Fourier, was embedded in the universe at all levels. All things naturally work together for good. In particular, he taught that there is a principle of harmony in human nature and that, if this innate harmony is allowed to have free course, men become virtuous and happy both as individuals and in society. Misery and vice are results of the unnatural restraints that society imposes on the gratification of desire. Human nature attains to its full development when the passions are indulged without artificial restriction. Society should therefore be reconstructed so that the principle of harmony could be realized in all human relations.

Fourier had an intricate blue-print for the division of society into *phalanges* of about 1,600 persons each. Each *phalange* would occupy an area of land to be known as a *phalanstère*—a word that has found its way into the *Oxford English Dictionary* as "phalanstery". These communities would have appropriate buildings and a mixed and balanced constitution. The members would be able to vary their occupations according to taste. Fourier thus "believed that, when once the way had been shown by a few examples, human society would crystallise easily into a series of college-like communities, in which all things would be in common; where spells of work and play, industry and

---

[1] On Fourier, see *Selections from the works of Fourier* with an introduction by Charles Gide (E.T., 1901).

agriculture, education and the arts, would dovetail into one another without friction".[1] He extended this peculiar kind of communism to the institution of marriage.

It was because of its apparent hedonism, its optimistic view of human nature, and its inconsistency with Christian morality, that the followers of Buchez would have nothing to do with fourierism. As one of them put it:

> We have always considered that fourierism is the most complete and direct negation of all morality and of all Christianity and that the teaching of the phalansterians is infinitely dangerous for the whole of society.[2]

On the other hand, some of the fourierists themselves sought the collaboration of catholics, claiming that their doctrine, the science of harmony, was basically a theory of industrial organization, which was not necessarily bound up with Fourier's views about religion and morality, and that, as a theory of industrial organization, it was the proper corollary of Christianity. It was certainly the ideas of social harmony and of co-operation in industry that made fourierism attractive to some Christian socialists. The attitude of the Christian fourierists was that the Master's metaphysics and ethics were aberrational accessories to his doctrine of social relations, much as to-day there are Christian freudians who adopt Freud's psychology without his philosophy.

The Christian fourierists were a mixed bag of individual social catholics. They cannot be said to have constituted a school like the buchezians.[3] M. Duroselle instances a number of individuals who can be classified as fourierists: they include a lecturer in mathematics, a naval officer, an architect, a priest-journalist, and some men of letters. They all appear to have been intellectuals

---

[1] J. H. Clapham, *Economic Development of France and Germany; 1815–1914* (1921), p. 266.

[2] See Duroselle, p. 126.

[3] "On peut parler des Fouriéristes catholiques et non du Fouriérisme catholique." Duroselle, p. 120.

who harboured Christian socialist ideas, for which they acknowledged their indebtedness to Fourier. I will take the case of one
of them, Hippolyte de la Morvonnais (1802–53),[1] who may
be accepted as fairly representative of the type.

La Morvonnais was a Breton like Lamennais and a poet like
Maurice de Guèrin. In 1824, at the age of twenty-two, he
abandoned both the study of law and the catholic faith, and
went to live in Paris where he became associated with a literary
circle that was impregnated with romanticism, liberalism, and
scepticism. Then, after his marriage in 1826, he returned to
Brittany where he lived the life of a country gentleman and
leisured man of letters. But he was increasingly haunted by a
nostalgia for the faith. It was in consequence of visits to Lamennais' house at La Chesnaie (of which he has left on record
charming and detailed accounts),[2] and of the profound impression made upon him by Lamennais and Gerbet, that La Morvonnais regained his faith. Thus it was liberal catholicism, not
the catholicism of Gregory XVI, that drew him back to the
Church, and he remained a liberal catholic till the end of his life.

From 1840, however, when he became acquainted with the
doctrine of Fourier and fell under its spell, he was more concerned about social regeneration or social reform than about
political liberty. He accepted fourierism because it seemed to him
to be the only school of socialism that was not revolutionary, or
that was pacific and not violent in its methods, and also because
it stood for the introduction of socialism gradually and by local
experiments. That particularly appealed to him because he hoped
to initiate such an experiment himself in his own commune.

He was fond of saying that fourierism, the application of the
principle of harmony to social relations, was fundamentally
nothing else than catholic teaching formulated and developed.
Indeed, he went so far as to compare Fourier with Christ as the

[1] See E. Fleury, op cit.; Duroselle, pp. 139–47.
[2] See Fleury, op. cit., pp. 118–35.

human and divine founders of Christian socialism. The clearest explanation of his position is to be found in an article on Christian socialism which he prepared but did not publish. A few quotations from this will indicate his point of view. He allowed that the word "socialism" like the word "religion" could have a good and a bad sense. In the good sense,

> socialism means the doctrine of co-operation; it is a doctrine that aims at substituting co-operation for individualism. But what can be more Christian than co-operation? Christianity, in all its utterances and in all respects, engages us to co-operate with one another... If we neglect this sentiment which Christianity plants and develops in our hearts, we become infidels; we have faith without the most important works of our divine religion, the works of charity....
>
> Applied socialism would carry Christian inspiration into legislation, and would give us evangelical institutions, whereas the liberal system, because it tends to division, has the effect of carrying egoism into institutions... Christianity ought to intervene with all its strength, for it protects man's personality and the social existence of the family. It does so because it recognizes a law and a legislator which are above the law that emanates from majorities... It defends the weak against the strong, and takes in hand before every other cause the cause of the weak and the afflicted....
>
> Socialism viewed in a Christian light and inspired by the Gospel gives us a more perfect society than liberalism... with its device "every man for himself"... The legislation of the liberal system guarantees only our liberty, which is all right for those who have no need to earn their living, but offers no guarantee to those who depend for support on work, without which liberty can be no more than an empty word.[1]

It was a common theme of the social catholics—as distinguished from the liberals or upholders of *laissez faire*—that liberty was of no use to men who were dying of hunger.

La Morvonnais pictured in romantic language and in

[1] See ibid., pp. 301ff.

22

comprehensive terms a society in which universal peace and harmony would be achieved. When he was charged with being utopian in his expectations, he replied that at the close of the ancient world the abolition of slavery had been regarded as impossible, and that when the age of feudalism was coming to an end serfdom was regarded as an essential social condition.

> Now that our juridical and commercial civilization is giving way to one that will be characterized by the Christian organization of labour and the creation of an evangelical society, it is asserted that the progressive transformation of workers with no assured wages into workers whose remuneration will be assured and proportionate to their work is an impossibility and a danger that threatens to reduce everything to chaos.—In similar periods the same kind of thing is always said. [1]

Sincere as was La Morvonnais' conversion to catholicism, he allowed Fourier's teaching to modify his religious beliefs as well as his social doctrines. For example, he did not accept the dogmas of either original sin or everlasting punishment, but as he was a layman these heterodoxies were tolerated. I shall have occasion to refer to him again.

I have said that conservatives as well as socialists had a part in the development of social catholicism. It had a right wing as well as a left wing. But before taking a further look at the social catholicism of the right before 1848, I want to glance at a group that was intermediate between the right and the left—the "liberal catholics". These were catholics who had been in sympathy with the ideas of the *Avenir* and who, after its condemnation and Lamennais' break with the Church, did not abandon the hope of reconciling catholicism with the cause of political liberty.

As we have seen, the *Avenir* and its collaborators, with the exception of de Coux and Gerbet, had not been directly concerned with the evils of industrialism. The liberties they had

[1] See ibid., pp. 521f.

espoused had not included the liberation of the proletariat from industrial slavery. After the departure of Lamennais, the chief task which the liberal catholics set themselves was the struggle for educational liberty, that is, freedom for the Church to establish schools outside the State University system. It was apparently easy to be so absorbed in that struggle as to be blind to the need of the working class for tolerable conditions of life. That was the case, for instance, with Montalembert who combined liberal politics with social conservatism. It has been said of him that "during the whole of his career he only once concerned himself with labour problems".[1]

While there were other liberal catholics who showed more awareness of the problems, they did not as a group get beyond recognizing the duty of charity and almsgiving and the need to foster the spirit of reconciliation between classes and parties. The desire to exercise a reconciling influence and to translate charity into action was conspicuous in Frédéric Ozanam (1813–53)[2] who stands out in this group by the saintliness of his character, by his consecration to the service of the poor, and by his foundation of the Society of St Vincent de Paul.[3]

As a student in Paris he was inspired by the lectures of de Coux and Gerbet, and he formed an association with other students which aimed at deepening their understanding of the catholic faith and their corporate devotion and at doing practical works of mercy. This was the origin of the Society of St Vincent de Paul which was "founded in order to sustain young people in the faith by the practice of charity".[4] It was organized in branches known as "conferences", which were established in the principal cities of France.[5] Its members were in particular pledged to visit

[1] Duroselle, p. 158.

[2] On Ozanam, see L. Baunard, *Frédéric Ozanam d'après sa correspondance* (1914).

[3] See J. Brodrick, s.j., *Frédéric Ozanam and his society* (1933).

[4] See Duroselle, p. 175.

[5] E.g. for Toulouse, see P. Droulers, s.j., *Action pastorale et problèmes sociaux sous la monarchie de juillet* (1954), pp. 320–31.

the poor in their homes and to make friends with whole families. It was a kind of catholic student movement with a number of auxiliary agencies. Linked with it, for example, were societies for the care of apprentices and of domestic servants.

Ozanam himself and most of his associates were more or less legitimist in their political sentiments: they desired a restoration of the Bourbon monarchy and a positively catholic government. At any rate, they viewed with repugnance the rule of Louis Philippe, the citizen king, and the liberal *bourgeoisie* upon which it depended. It is the case, broadly speaking, that social catholicism, in the period from 1830 to 1848, secured its recruits not from supporters of the July monarchy, but from those who disliked it: the democrats and republicans, on the one hand, and the legitimists or conservatives, on the other.

Real concern about the crying evils of industrialism was no doubt exceptional among the conservative catholics. Our preoccupation here with social catholicism should not be allowed to obscure the fact that the majority of educated French catholics at this time, and for long afterwards, were either indifferent to social questions or simply reactionary. Thus, Count Molé, when he took his place in the *Académie Française* in 1840, could speak of the clergy as the "sublime guardian of public order", and a certain Abbé Luc, in a book entitled, *De la question du paupérisme sous le point de vue politique et social* (1842), wrote: "Poverty, considered as the necessary lot of the larger part of mankind, is by no means an evil ... It serves as a basis for authority, increases courage, shows up merit, works marvels, and is useful and advantageous to government." Guizot spoke of the Church as "the naturally ally, the necessary support, of every government", and he had ample warrant for doing so.[1] Nevertheless,

---

[1] For the quotations in the text, see Poupard, op. cit., pp. 108f. Cp. his quotation on p. 110 about the attitude of the papal internuncio in Paris.

there was a distinct school of conservative social catholics. Its existence can be accounted for in the following ways.

First, among the members of the privileged classes who until 1830 had been ardent supporters of the Restoration monarchy, a substantial number had had a charitable interest in the welfare of the poor,[1] and this interest did not disappear or evaporate with the Bourbons. It sought a new outlet.

Secondly, the conservatives sincerely believed in the merits of the *ancien régime* and especially of the pre-revolutionary corporations or trade and professional guilds, and they contrasted the benefits which those institutions had conferred on the body politic with the evils that resulted from an individualistic view of man and the isolation of the workers. In other words, they saw themselves as heirs of a social tradition that they could seek to commend.

Thirdly, the conservatives were legitimists at heart and were naturally always on the look-out for ammunition with which to attack the July régime. The popular discontent with it, the worsened conditions of the working class, and the outbreaks of disorder which from time to time were their consequence, were all arguments that legitimists had no disposition to neglect. Some of them saw that they could do so with integrity only if their sympathy with the victims of what they denounced was active and genuine. "Ministers of liberalism, we shall defend the poor against you!" declared a conservative journal. "The men of the right are the real protectors of the people."[2]

Finally, Count de Falloux (author of the famous *loi Falloux*), in his *Mémoires d'un royaliste*, suggests a further reason for the interest of legitimists in social service, namely that there was not any other public activity in which they were free to engage.

The legitimist part cannot be denied the merit of having brought the most numerous contingent to the *œuvres* which were started at

---

[1] Cp. p. 3 above.   [2] See Duroselle, p. 201.

this time (i.e. under the July régime). They were excluded, and indeed excluded themselves, from participation in politics, but they wanted to rebut the reproach of escapism that was levelled against them. They realized that a large and fruitful field of action could still be open to them in social service.[1]

The energies of the conservative social catholics were mostly occupied in organizing charitable activities for the benefit of the workers. But some of them went further and attempted a criticism of the structure of industrial society and proposed specific reforms such as the revival of guilds, legislation to regulate child labour and hours of work, and improved housing.

The most interesting and influential member of this group of legitimists was Count Armand de Melun (1807–77),[2] whose rôle might be compared to that of Lord Shaftesbury in England. He was an aristocrat who succeeded in making himself an authentic mouthpiece of the workers. He was primarily a man of action. He had been impressed by the *Avenir*, and had become a member of the circle that met in the *salon* of Madame Swetchine, Lacordaire's friend. She introduced him to Sœur Rosalie, a dedicated Daughter of Charity, who drew many of the well-to-do into the service of the poor, among whom she worked in one of the most derelict districts of Paris. De Melun said of her:

> Until then, I had never visited anyone who was poor, I knew only those who had held out their hands to me in the streets . . . I had hitherto regarded it as the job of public assistance and welfare offices to get to know them and to provide relief for them. . . . Such being my attitude, the life lived by Sœur Rosalie among these poor people came upon me as the revelation of an unknown world that laid hold of me.[3]

De Melun considered the possibility of a vocation to the priesthood. In fact the Archbishop of Paris (Affre) wanted to

---

[1] De Falloux, op. cit. (4th ed., 1888), i, 167.
[2] On de Melun, see Duroselle, pp. 209–17.
[3] See Duroselle, p. 212.

make him his vicar-general and promised to ordain him without his having to undergo training in a seminary, but de Melun was convinced that, if the workers were to be won back to Christianity, the laity must be the advance-guard of God's army and that his place was there.

Among his achievements was the formation of something like a charity organization society, which prevented wasteful overlapping and ill-advised forms of charity. It set itself to study scientifically the best methods of serving the poor and of improving their conditions. He also founded a journal, *Annales de la Charité*, which served as an organ for the discussion of these questions and for the diffusion of good ideas. Villeneuve-Bargemont collaborated with him in this.

De Melun came to be acknowledged as the spokesman of the unenfranchised workers, and he and Villeneuve-Bargemont even succeeded in making Parliament give its attention to social problems. In the course of a remarkable speech in the Chamber of Deputies in 1840, Villeneuve-Bargemont declared that the great problem of the age was how to raise the condition of the long-suffering working class.

> It is time seriously to set about its solution, and to grapple with the task of realizing a true social economy, which is too often lost sight of amid our sterile political agitations.[1]

De Melun himself was not in Parliament, but he made an impact there by preparing factual information and concrete proposals for reform, for example, with regard to the law about child labour.

The official spokesmen of the Church, the bishops, were nearly all conservatives who sprang from the aristocratic and intellectual classes, and who had little or no perception of social problems. Among the few exceptions was Mgr Pierre Giraud (1791–1850), Archbishop of Cambrai in the industrial north. In

[1] Ibid., p. 231.

1845 he issued a Lenten pastoral letter on the "Law of Labour", which did reveal an awareness of what was going on, and which was welcomed by a socialist in these words:

> This is a generous, eloquent and bold utterance to come from an archbishop; here is social criticism, such as we have been making for fifteen years, making its appearance in Christian pulpits. We readily overlook certain reckless statements about ourselves . . . in order to applaud the honest indignation of his language.[1]

All this may not amount to much. The point is that before 1848 there was, amid the general blindness or indifference of the conservative classes, a minority that was keenly alive to the plight of the industrial masses.

Last but not least, before we come to the Revolution of 1848, I must say something about the Society of St Francis Xavier. This was founded in 1840 and was so named because of its missionary character: it was an anticipation of the "France, pays de mission" idea. Unlike the Society of St Vincent de Paul and its auxiliary agencies, which were for the service of youth, this society was for adult workers. While its primary object was to win them to the practice of religion and to provide opportunities for instruction, devotion, and Christian fellowship, it assumed a larger and more definitely social character. For this reason, and also because there were a good many legitimists among its members, it was viewed with suspicion by the government authorities. Documents exist which illustrate the attempts of the police to get the Archbishop of Paris to see that the society confined itself to purely religious and parochial activities. But Mgr Affre, who, as we have already seen, had social catholic

---

[1] Ibid., p. 240. For other bishops who showed themselves to be alive to the social problem, see Paul Droulers on "Des évêques parlent de la question ouvrière en France avant 1848" (art.), *Revue de l'Action Populaire* (April 1961), pp. 442–60.

sympathies, was adroit and resourceful in protecting the society from interference.

The Society of St Francis Xavier consisted of workers who had to be proposed for membership by existing members. Monthly meetings were held in churches. (It would have been illegal to hold such meetings elsewhere under the July régime.) After vespers the minutes of the previous meeting were read, and there were discussions and lectures, interspersed with hymn singing. Religious instruction was given by priests, and moral instruction by laymen. The regular participation of laymen in giving lectures and instruction was a feature of the society's meetings which made the police suspect that it had a subversive tendency, and certainly some of the speakers did give radical and socialistic teaching.

From 1842 members paid a small subscription, and became entitled to medical treatment and support in case of illness. In fact, it became a friendly society with free legal aid, funeral benefits, and so on. The society spread from Paris to other cities and towns. In Paris it had about 6,000 members in 1843, and two years later the number had risen to 15,000. There were 3,000 members at Lyons in 1845.[1]

The most prominent personality in the society was François-Auguste Ledreuille (1797–1860). He was of humble birth and had been a worker himself before he was ordained deacon in 1819, but he subsequently abandoned an ecclesiastical career and became a professor of philosophy and literature. Little is known about his manner of life until in 1843 he came to the fore as a frequent and popular lay speaker at the meetings of the Society of St Francis Xavier.

Mgr Affre was so impressed by his gifts of oratory and leadership that he persuaded him to proceed to the priesthood, which he did in 1845. Ledreuille was henceforth known as "the Workers' Priest" or as "le Père des Ouvriers". His first mass was

[1] On the Society of St Francis Xavier, see Duroselle, pt. I, ch. 5.

celebrated in Notre Dame, and the *Univers* published an account of it:

> This new apostle of the people celebrated his first mass last Sunday amid an immense concourse of the faithful among whom there was a large number of the members of the Society of St Francis Xavier. At the communion long files of working men came forward to take their place at the altar rail. . . . The crowd was much moved, and recalled how in the midst of a society rotten with materialism, as ours is, Christianity had through men of the people marched to the conquest of the world.[1]

Ledreuille preached on this occasion to the workers, and in the course of his sermon, said:

> The Church, in the person of the wise, pious and venerable pontiff who governs this great diocese . . . has cast its eyes on me, a man of the people, in order to honour the people in my person; and making an exception which is entirely due to you, he consecrated me as a priest, dispensing me, on your account, from the formalities and tests that are ordinarily necessary.[2]

A few days later Ledreuille preached to a wealthy congregation in another church, and warned them in strong language that, if they did not give heed promptly to the crying needs of the working class, they would deserve the vengeance that would be meted out to them. The prefect of police, in making a report on this sermon, accused Ledreuille of holding "extremely impassioned and dangerous anti-monarchist opinions" and of having assigned himself "the mission of exciting and stirring up the working class".[3]

Ledreuille extended the influence of the Society of St Francis Xavier in Paris by establishing in 1844 a "Maison des Ouvriers" which was both an employment bureau and a settlement that was day by day able to provide ampler services for workers than the Society itself. At the same time he took steps to restrain the

[1] See ibid., pp. 267f.   [2] Ibid., p. 268.   [3] Ibid., p. 269.

flow of workers from the provinces into the metropolis, since that only increased the unemployment problem. In 1848 he was able to claim to have been of service to more than 100,000 families. A monthly journal was published, the *Revue du Travail*. It was produced and distributed by unemployed workers and offered a useful news service to workers generally.

It is clear that the Society of St Francis Xavier and the Maison des Ouvriers had a notable influence and contributed to the popularity of the Church at the time of the 1848 Revolution. A good deal more research, however, needs to be done before the extent and the grounds of the Church's popularity then can be properly assessed.[1] Inferences have been too easily drawn from the blessing of trees of liberty by the parish clergy. However, there is no doubt that the Church did have considerable prestige with the people at this critical moment, and it is highly probable that this last manifestation of incipient social catholicism had something to do with it.

[1] See F. Isambert, "L'attitude religieuse des ouvriers français au milieu du XIXe siècle" (art.), *Archives de Sociologie des Religions* (1958), vi, 7–35.

2

France: The Second Republic

The Revolution of February 1848 in its first phase was welcomed by catholics generally, even by the conservative hierarchy of the Church. Nearly everyone seems to have been carried away by the idyllic atmosphere—"bien romantique, et bien française"[1]— which for a few weeks united all citizens and all classes in a common enthusiasm. Not only did this revolution, unlike that of 1830, appear to be friendly to the Church, but the conservative or legitimist catholics, who realized that there was no present possibility of a Bourbon restoration or of a renewed alliance between the altar and the throne, were disposed to welcome any régime that promised greater liberty for the Church, especially in the field of education—the particular liberty for which they had been campaigning without success during the reign of Louis Philippe.

So we find the ultramontane Louis Veuillot (1813–83), in the *Univers* (26 February 1848), declaring that the divine right of kings was a gallican doctrine, whereas catholic theology proclaims the divine right of peoples.

The Europe of the middle ages was a confederation of Christian democracies. The legislation of the popes and councils was a legislation of liberty. The whole history of the Christian world for ten centuries is nothing but the story of the struggles for Christian liberty represented by the Church against the reactions and

[1] Duroselle in *Revue d'Histoire de l'Église de France* (1948), p. 45.

enterprises of pagan despotism. What else is there to be seen all the way from the cross of Jesus Christ to the throne of Pius IX . . .?[1]

Likewise Montalembert, who in the preceding month had electrified and delighted his fellow peers by a speech in which he had violently attacked radicalism as the greatest of all threats, and who paradoxically had been as much appalled by the February Revolution as he had been enchanted by that of July, was nevertheless moved to write in the *Univers*:

> The catholics will descend . . . into the arena, with all their fellow-citizens, there to claim all the political and social liberties that will henceforth be the indefeasible patrimony of France. They will descend to fulfil a sacred duty, a national duty, a Christian duty. They will take with them an unlimited trust in the empenetrable designs of God, an ardent love for the Fatherland, an imperishable devotion to its glory and honour.[2]

The bishops, almost with one accord,[3] saluted the Republic, and announced that it represented the triumph of liberty, fraternity, and equality, which had been the principles of the Gospel of Jesus Christ for 1,800 years (or words to that effect), thus using a language which was the precise opposite of what customarily fell from their lips. Here is just one example. Mgr Pierre-Louis Parisis (1795–1866), Bishop of Langres, who was later to be a leading ultramontane conservative, welcomed the February Revolution in these terms:

> There is nothing more profoundly—indeed, I would say more exclusively—Christian than these three words that are inscribed on the national flag: LIBERTY, EQUALITY, FRATERNITY. Far from repudiating these sublime words, Christianity claims them as its own work, its own creation: it is Christianity, and Christianity alone, that has introduced them, that has consecrated them, and caused them to be practised in the world . . . What therefore we

---

[1] See G. Bazin, *Vie de Mgr Maret*, i, 209.
[2] See Lecanuet, *Montalembert*, ii, 386.
[3] For many examples see Bazin, op. cit., vol. i, ch. xv.

ought to ask of God before everything else, dear brethren, what we ought to ask of him urgently, is that everyone may truly understand and love this glorious slogan: LIBERTY, EQUALITY, FRATERNITY.[1]

These favourable episcopal reactions to the Revolution were inspired by the hopeful and intoxicating emotion that was in the air. The Revolution had not been prepared for, and it had taken people generally by surprise, so that no one could be sure what to expect and all were inclined to hope for the best. Few catholics at first perceived the ambiguity of the Revolution's motivation. It had been motivated both by the desire of the lesser *bourgeoisie* for a wider distribution of political power and by the determination of the Parisian proletariat to secure tolerable conditions of living and working. That is to say, it was in the intention of its promoters both a political and a social revolution.

In the provisional government these antithetic interests were combined. A struggle between them was latent from the beginning. The social character of the Revolution was illustrated by the decree of 25 February 1848 guaranteeing the right to work, and it was followed by the establishment of the "national workshops" to provide work for the unemployed. But, even by the time that the elections to the Constituent Assembly took place two months later, it was evident that the radically democratic and socialist elements in the revolution had already been checked. Out of 880 candidates elected not more than thirty were workers, and not more than 100 were socialists. The generality were members of the *bourgeoisie* and professional classes, who might equally well have been elected under the previous régime.[2]

The leaders of the proletariat did not quietly sit down under this reverse. There was a critical demonstration on 15 May 1848 when the Constituent Assembly was invaded by the populace,

[1] Ibid., i, 198f.
[2] See Jean Dautry, *Histoire de la Révolution de 1848 en France* (1948), pt. II, ch. vi.

and in June there was the fateful rising of the Parisian workers which was set off by the Government's decision to close the national workshops. The insurrection was ruthlessly crushed by General Cavaignac, and it was then that the archbishop (Affre) lost his life when trying to separate the combatants.

The honeymoon period of the Revolution was over. The conservative republicans and the "Party of Order" were now in the ascendant. Louis Napoleon, who was playing his cards with consummate skill, was already on the scene, and the way was being prepared for the *coup d'état* of December 1851. It is with this course of events in mind that we must look at the development of social catholicism in 1848 and under the Second Republic.

At the outset, during the honeymoon period, the prospects of the Christian socialists or Christian democrats seemed bright indeed. The stream was flowing fast in the direction of a new social order, in which there might be a synthesis of socialism with catholicism. Thus Armand de Melun wrote in his *Mémoires*:

> As regards the study and solution of the social questions which we had pursued during the reign of Louis Philippe, and which had only with much difficulty and at the last moment won the attention of the Government of July, the Revolution of 1848 seemed at first to promise real progress. At last what we regarded as the principal and most urgent object of politics was going to have its proper place, namely, the amelioration of the lot of the people who had now become sovereign.[1]

Buchez, who became first President of the Constituent Assembly, Ozanam, and others felt the same. But this promising outlook did not last long, and the social catholics soon had to moderate their hopes and to limit their objectives. One result of the reactionary atmosphere after the June insurrection was to separate the social catholics of the left (the genuine republicans and democrats) from those with a conservative and legitimist

[1] See Duroselle, *Débuts*, p. 292.

36

background and outlook, and it is necessary to consider them apart.

I turn first then to the activities of the Christian democrats in 1848. Just as Lamennais had met the July Revolution by starting the *Avenir*, so the Christian democrats now took advantage of the new freedom of the press to start a similar daily paper in order to propagate their ideas. This was the *Ère Nouvelle*, which like the *Avenir* lasted for about a year. The initiative was taken by Abbé Henri-Louis-Charles Maret (1805–84) and Ozanam. Maret was a professor of theology in the university, and he was later to become prominent on account of his determined gallicanism. When Napoleon III nominated him to a diocesan bishopric, the pope refused to accept the nomination, and Maret had to be fobbed off with a titular see *in partibus infidelium*. As a youth Maret had been won to sympathy with liberal and democratic ideas. Now he wrote:

> Fraternity is for us only the evangelical love of the neighbour passing into laws and morals; we look upon the progressive amelioration of the moral and material condition of the working class as the very end of society.[1]

As regards Ozanam, he had, just before the February Revolution, published a striking article in the *Correspondant*, the journal of the liberal catholics, in which he had used the expression "Passons aux barbares",[2] "let us turn to the barbarians", by which he explained that he meant:

> we should turn from the camp of the kings and statesmen of 1815 ... to go to the people ... that we should occupy ourselves with the people who have too many needs and not enough rights, who claim with reason a fuller part in public affairs, guarantees for work and against distress ...[3]

[1] See ibid., pp. 295f.
[2] For other associations of this expression, see Isambert, *Christianisme et classe ouvrière*, p. 201.   [3] See Duroselle, p. 296.

Maret and Ozanam secured the concurrence of Lacordaire who became the editor of the *Ère Nouvelle*. Other collaborators included Charles de Coux and Charles Sainte-Foi (1805–61),[1] both former mennaisians. Mgr Affre wrote a letter of commendation. Montalembert, despite his lack of enthusiasm for the Revolution, proposed to Lacordaire that he should write for the *Ère Nouvelle*, but Lacordaire repulsed him with the brusque remark; "It is impossible: you are *un vaincu*."[2] (This was an allusion to Montalembert's speech against the radicals in the previous month, when he had spoken of the representatives of order as having been vanquished in the civil war in Switzerland.) Montalembert therefore collaborated in the *Univers* and in the *parti catholique* with Veuillot with whom he was now on friendly terms, although he was not to remain so.

Of the *parti catholique*, which had held the catholics together under the July monarchy in the struggle for educational liberty, Maret said at this time:

This party has concerned itself only with religious liberty and to some extent with liberty of association; it has been unwilling to recognize that all liberties are connected and interdependent. It has shown but little interest in the condition of the disinherited classes.[3]

In the course of its prospectus, the *Ère Nouvelle* said:

We see with sorrow the moral and physical hardships of so many of our brothers who bear here below the heaviest part of the world's work, a part that has become still more oppressive through the development of industry and civilization. We do not believe that these evils are incapable of being remedied. While none of the children of men can escape suffering, charity wedded to science can all the same do something to reduce its incidence, even if it cannot stop it altogether. The Church has always worked to that end; in no period has she lost sight of the poor, and now more than ever, if that be possible, because of the new and strange ills that beset the

---

[1] As regards the latter, see my book, *Prophecy and Papacy*, pp. 143f.
[2] See Duroselle, p. 297; cp. Lecanuet, op. cit., ii, 365.
[3] See Duroselle, p. 295.

world, she has her eyes and her heart on the wounds of humanity. We expect, we must expect, the Republic to use its power to relieve the miseries of the largest number of its children.[1]

So far as circulation went, the *Ère Nouvelle* had a promising start. Within a fortnight it had over 2,000 subscribers, and by the end of June the circulation was 20,000, which was very considerable for that time. Editorially, its progress was less happy. Lacordaire was not prepared to go so far as Maret and Ozanam, either politically or socially. He was not a convinced republican or democrat. In the idiom of the period, he was a republican of the morrow: that is, he was prepared to see what could be made of the new régime, though he preferred a limited monarchy.

However, he let himself be elected a member of the Constituent Assembly, where he not only appeared in his white Dominican habit but took his seat among the extreme republicans. He was warmly received and indeed had a popular ovation. Lacordaire's biographer (Foisset) said that it was by decision of the board of the *Ère Nouvelle* that he took his seat on the extreme left, but this appears to be a mistake. It was Lacordaire's own decision. But he soon found that he was embarrassed by his apparent identification with the extreme republicans, especially after the humiliating invasion of the Assembly by the populace on 15 May. But to change his seat and place himself among the monarchists would cause further embarrassment and misunderstanding.[2] So he resigned after a bare fortnight in the Assembly.

It may be that he found he had little aptitude or taste for the rough and tumble of political warfare, which he felt to be inconsistent with his vocation as a religious. Perhaps too, like some other great preachers, he was happier in the security of the pulpit than in the cut and thrust of debate, though he had had a legal training. Anyhow, he wanted at the same time to retire from the editorship of the *Ère Nouvelle*, but he was persuaded to continue for the time being.

[1] See Bazin, op. cit., i, 231f.   [2] Ibid., i, 246ff.

Meanwhile, in its pages Maret and Ozanam had been vigorously espousing the cause of the workers, extolling the social character of the Revolution, and affirming that beside individual charity there should be "another movement inspired by Christianity"[1] which would tend to equalize conditions and ensure a more equitable distribution of this world's goods. They advocated a reduction in the hours of work, and a graduated income-tax instead of the taxation of goods, which bore hardly on the workers. But at the same time other contributors to the paper were allowed to criticize these proposals.

The *Ère Nouvelle* adopted a sympathetic attitude to the insurgents of June, while deploring their doctrines. "Most of them", it said, "were workers driven to desperation by the poverty and hunger that had beset them for four months." Ozanam, while granting that there was bound to be suffering and hardship in this world, went on to say that

> the whole effort of the present century, the whole genius of our three revolutions, the whole price of so much blood shed, can be only the relief of the suffering classes ... We want statesmen to use all their enterprise to that most desirable end, and however little we may have accomplished so far by our appeals, we shall give no rest to the Government or to the National Assembly.[2]

However, the *Ère Nouvelle* spoke with various voices until the beginning of September when Lacordaire resigned the editorship and was succeeded by Maret. A stronger line was now taken both in attacking the *bourgeoisie* and in advocating such social principles as the right to work. Maret also recruited some new collaborators whose social catholicism was more definite and keen. He aimed at forming a school of social catholics who would discriminate between what was true and false in current social and economic theory and be able to propagate a policy that could outdo its rivals. "Is it not a deplorable spectacle", he

[1] See Duroselle, p. 302.   [2] Ibid., p. 306.

asked, "to see the catholics always on the defensive, when they ought to be taking the initiative in all truly progressive movements? What is the good of refuting the pseudo-socialists? Let us make socialists ourselves."[1]

By the beginning of 1849 the *Ère Nouvelle* was running into difficulties, as the *Avenir* had done. The circulation was reduced to 3,200, when it needed 4,000 subscribers in order to pay its way. The bishops disapproved and penalized priests who, they heard, were subscribing to it.[2] One of them wrote in response to a prospectus of the paper that had been sent to him in October 1848:

> I desire neither for myself nor my brethren, the clergy, this enthusiastic *rupture with the past, these aspirations towards a new social organization,* which, according to the prospectus before me, *are the* raison d'être *of the journal which it recommends.*[3]

As regards the influence that had been exerted by the *Ère Nouvelle* and the circles it had reached, we can have no better testimony than that of the editor of its rival, the *Univers.* On 2 December 1848 Louis Veuillot wrote:

> The *Ère Nouvelle* is called to do a good work which the other catholic papers cannot do: its words reach areas which their words do not reach. The recent revival of religious feeling has drawn, and is still drawing every day, out of the parties that were formerly hostile to the Church, and making catholics of them, men who are naturally more advanced and more progressive than their brothers. These men had no newspaper; they have one now, and in our view it would have been a real misfortune if this organ had been taken away from them; for it has their confidence in a way that the older papers cannot have, following as they do lines that are not contrary but different.[4]

---

[1] Ibid., p. 315.
[2] See Bazin, op. cit., i, 317.
[3] See Duroselle, p. 316.
[4] See Bazin, op. cit., i, 249.

These were generous words, but they were not echoed by others who might have been expected to be more sympathetic. In October 1848 Abbé Félix Dupanloup (1802–78), the future Bishop of Orleans, had bought the paper *Ami de la Religion* with a view to making it an organ more liberal than the *Univers* and less dangerous than the *Ère Nouvelle*. Montalembert, who was associated with Dupanloup, proceeded to publish in the *Ami de la Religion* what was in effect a violent and most injurious attack on the *Ère Nouvelle* and all it stood for.[1]

All these things were against it, as well as the general trend to political reaction. On 25 March 1849—again as in the case of the *Avenir*—the proprietors of the *Ère Nouvelle*—Maret, Ozanam, and Arnaud de l'Ariège (the ablest of their new recruits)—addressed an appeal to the pope. It should be remembered that it was still possible to regard Pio Nono as a liberal. Speaking of themselves in the third person, they said:

> The immortal work of conciliating liberty with religion, Holy Father, which is the glory of your pontificate . . ., has been their inspiration. They have dared, they have determined, to follow in the footsteps of their father and their supreme pastor. To prove to the people that there is no true liberty without religion, and that modern civilization, which has sprung from Christianity, will perish, unless it acquires new vigour from the sources in which it originated, this has been the conviction that has animated all their work. . . .
>
> A close study of the moral and social condition of our country convinced us that France has arrived at *the age of political liberty and equality*, and we have not been afraid . . . to accept *democracy* and to enter into an alliance with it.[2]

But there was no need for the pope to reply to this appeal. The paper could not go on as it was. It had now only 2,500 subscribers, and financial difficulties made it necessary to dispose of it. It was sold to a legitimist who pretended that he would

[1] Ibid., i, 273.   [2] Ibid., i, 351ff.

maintain its policy, but who really wanted it as an organ of the royalist cause. So it passed out of the hands of these democratic social catholics, and they were thus deprived of an organ and a rallying point.

There were other social catholics of the left, priests and lay-men, who were engaged in journalism at this period, both in Paris and in the provinces. Some were disciples of Buchez, others of Fourier or Proudhon. They proclaimed socialism as a corol-lary of the Gospel and advocated State action, or co-operation by the workers, as the case might be. M. Duroselle has collected evidence of their activities. I will cite just one specimen of their oratory, from a journal that was published by a group in Lyons. The style is reminiscent of Lamennais.

> Priests of Jesus Christ, you have before you a magnificent task. Hitherto you have taught the salvation of the individual. It is time to teach the salvation of society . . . You have often spoken to the people of hope and of resignation, too seldom of their rights. Often you have said that destitution is the daughter of vice; too seldom that it is also the result of social evil. Often your charity has relieved their hardships, too rarely has it looked for institutions to cure poverty. This is why the people disregard you. Others than you will lead them, and to-day, when you preach the morality of your Master, the people believe that you are serving the interests of their oppressors. [1]

In addition to journalism, there were some practical experi-ments, such as co-operative societies. And there was the Christian commune founded by Hippolyte de la Morvonnais, to which he consecrated the last years of his life (he died in 1853). La Morvonnais, as we have seen, had been a catholic fourierist since about 1840. He retained his admiration for Fourier's genius, but he parted company from most of his fellow disciples on the ground, as he said, that they lacked two essential qualities— "poetic charm and religious grace".[2] These are not exactly

[1] See Duroselle, p. 373.   [2] Ibid., p. 383.

the most valuable assets to be looked for in social reformers, but La Morvonnais himself was a poet and a romantic.

He substituted for Fourier's idea of the "phalange" that of the Christian commune as the basis of a new social order. The social order, he said, should be modelled on the image of the Christian family in which all the members help one another. In the Christian commune all the families of which it is composed should help one another as the members of a family do. In each commune there would be administrative, educational, and religious institutions which would ensure that all the members fairly participated in the necessary elements of social life. He realized that his scheme was chiefly appropriate to rural and agricultural conditions. It would be of no particular interest, if it had been only a blue-print in his mind, but he did make a real attempt to translate it into practice.

He did this in the district of Brittany where his home was (Guildo). He sought to get a number of villages or hamlets combined into a new commune. The Bishop of St Brieuc constituted them as a new ecclesiastical parish. The foundation stone of the church was laid on 26 February 1848, just when the Republic was being proclaimed. Although a large majority of the inhabitants signed a petition in favour of the scheme, the negotiations for the formation of a new civil commune encountered protracted difficulties on account of local jealousies and the fluctuations in the central administration in Paris. These negotiations had not come to a successful issue when La Morvonnais fell fatally ill. But that he had made a considerable impression on his compatriots in Brittany may be inferred from the fact that his funeral is reported to have taken place "amid an immense concourse of people from the neighbouring towns and country-side .... The whole population . . . waited upon the mortal remains of the good man who had been the founder of this parish and who had been blessed by all as a benefactor or as a friend."[1]

[1] Ibid., p. 391.

With La Morvonnais there was buried the last hope of an experimental realization of the catholic fourierist ideal. He had intended his Christian commune to be an exemplification of his social theories, and he had tried to get his friend, Arnaud de l'Ariège, to publicize the project in the National Assembly so that it might be acknowledged as a pattern of Christian socialism for all rural communities.

Something should be said about the Christian socialist priests of the period of the Second Republic. They were of course exceptional, but there were here and there priests who were not only republicans and socialists but also ecclesiastically more or less recalcitrant and even bumptious. With political and social radicalism they combined a critical attitude to the church hierarchy, and they protested against the despotic power which the bishops could wield over the inferior clergy. They claimed that, if parish priests enjoyed what in England is known as "the parson's freehold", they would be much more likely to identify themselves with the interests of the working class. As it was, if they showed any disposition of that kind, they were liable to incur severe episcopal displeasure and to be disciplined.

During the later period of the July monarchy, an example had been given to this type of priest by Abbé Clavel de Saint-Geniez. He had conducted a campaign on behalf of the rights of the inferior clergy, and had been in a good deal of trouble with his bishop. He edited a paper, entitled *Bien Social*, which while it was primarily addressed to the clergy and concerned with their affairs, also came out with genuine pieces of social catholicism. Clavel was a catholic follower of Fourier.

Why [he asked] do not our catholic pulpits, especially in the large towns, drop that wretched preoccupation with pennies and farthings which prevents the workers from gathering round then, and why do they not deal instead with the morality of work? . . . Does not

45

the religious education of the people deserve the attention of the episcopate at least as much as that of the aristocratic families? We have not yet come across a single utterance of our modern bishops that touches on this matter which is at this moment the concern of a million workers . . .[1]

As regards his reputed fourierism, Clavel said:

We are by no means fourierists, but we have read the works of Charles Fourier and we have often admired the great and generous ideas which he develops in them with regard to political economy and the humanitarian organization of society. His arguments are as ingenious as they are reasonable, so long as he does not lose himself in metaphysical digressions.[2]

That had been the line taken by other catholic fourierists. Clavel himself was not an original thinker, but he wanted to present himself as a sponsor of the interests of the people: so he picked up what social ideas he could. He urged the inferior clergy who, he said, were at all times in contact with the suffering masses, the most numerous portion of the family of Jesus Christ, to espouse the cause of agricultural colonies. But what could they do, when they were themselves in the state of helotry which the existing anti-Christian despotism imposed on them? It was utopian, he said, of the fourierists to suppose that they could create a new religion: they should attach their social policy to "the ancient religion of our fathers".

After the February Revolution, Clavel was active in the democratic clubs, and he came out with a more specific plea for socialism, which was to include, among other things, a national health service, the development of national workshops, and the utilization of unused châteaux as rest homes for the workers. "I say frankly", he declared, "that I am for eveything that is practicable in the various Christian socialist systems."[3]

Abbé Richard, assistant curate of Saint-Michel at Dijon, was

[1] Ibid., pp. 147f.　　[2] Ibid., p. 148.　　[3] Ibid., p. 150.

another priest of this kind. In January 1847 he had preached a sermon about the teaching of the Gospel concerning the rich and the poor. A local government official, reporting to headquarters on this sermon, said:

This is a perilous subject for the present time on account of its connection with communist doctrines, and only a superior and cultivated mind could handle it without getting into difficulties. But, far from avoiding them, the curate of Saint-Michel attacked them head on, and treated them not in order to extol charity, but in order to contrast the *rights* of the poor with the wealth of the rich. He said that the poor had a right to the superfluity of the rich, and that whatever the rich possessed that exceeded their basic needs was superfluity. He also attacked the dances and concerts which were got up to benefit the poor, claiming that by such charitable works the rich too easily set their conscience at rest, which they also did by imprisoning beggars in workhouses: out of sight, out of mind.[1]

The matter was referred to the bishop for him to handle. He suspended the curate for a month, and required him in future to submit his sermons to his superiors. To the government authorities the bishop wrote that only two expressions in Richard's sermons seemed inexcusable, "despite the authority of Massillon and M. de Lamennais who had inspired them". One was that in which he had protested in the name of the poor against the way some of the rich misused their wealth, a statement that smacked of communism; the other, that in which he had blamed the practice of shutting up mendicants in workhouses. This is typical of the attitude of the great majority of the bishops to any priest who was at all outspoken on social questions.

Some socialist priests went further than others and got into more serious trouble. For instance, Abbé de Montlouis, incumbent of Voussac in the diocese of Moulins, welcomed the 1848 Revolution with enthusiasm and, girt with a tricoloured

[1] Ibid., pp. 395f.

sash, blessed the tree of liberty. He started a club in the commune where he propagated a form of Christian socialism. He was soon inhibited by his bishop, but he refused to submit and went off to Paris where before long he was imprisoned for six months for subversive utterances.

Another priest (Abbé Percy), who was inhibited by his bishop, said that to bring over the inferior clergy to socialism it was only necessary to remove from the clerical code the articles which put a priest's future at the mercy of a despot (i.e. of his bishop). The priest who was free would shake off his old theological prejudices. He would quickly take his place on the route of social progress.

Mention must also be made of the banquet of socialist priests that was organized in Paris on 29 April 1849. Thirty-three priests were present, three in soutanes, the rest in lay clothes. There were 600 diners, most of them working men. Toasts were given to "Jesus of Nazareth the father of socialism" and to "the union of democracy and Christianity". One of the priests in the course of his speech said:

> Yes, citizens, I say this at the top of my voice, I am a republican socialist priest, one of those who are called red republicans; but also a catholic priest, for I intend to remain loyal to my faith and my religious duties. [Then turning to the working-men he added:] We want your emancipation, we will no longer allow the exploitation of man by man. It is time that the worker enjoyed all the fruit of his labour, and that an industrialist, only because he is a capitalist, should not fatten himself on your toil.[1]

These socialist priests were all silenced by their bishops in one way or another, sometimes at the request of the government authorities. It is interesting to note that Abbé Jacques-Paul Migne (1800–75), the editor and publisher of the famous *Patrologias* and of encyclopedias, helped some of these priests who were banned

---

[1] Ibid., pp. 399f.

by their bishops by giving them literary work to do. In one case at least he provided by this means a refuge for a priest who had married. Migne himself was an independent man of affairs, not of ideas. He does not himself seem to have had anything much in the way of social catholic sympathies. He was in fact not only a hard worker but a hard employer.

The social catholics of the left, whom we have been considering, were mostly freelances. After June 1848 they were disavowed not only by the episcopate but by the great mass of the faithful. They were also inclined to quarrel among themselves, as other Christian socialists have been known to do. Louis Napoleon's *coup d'état* of December 1851 dealt them a mortal blow. Duroselle's conclusion at this point is

> that with the Christian democrats there disappeared an original form of social catholicism that was hostile to the capitalist régime, favourable to a graduated income-tax, rightly or wrongly convinced that it was impossible to improve the conditions of the working class without a transformation of the social structure.[1]

We have yet to ask what the conservative social catholics were doing during the period of the Second Republic. After the first flush of welcome to the February Revolution, the Church as a whole, both clergy and laity, reverted to a thoroughly conservative attitude to both politics and the social question. The disorders and the insurrection that had followed the provisional government's radical social measures, such as the proclamation of the right to work and the establishment of national workshops, seemed to have discredited all schemes for social change, and to have underlined the importance of the Church's rôle as the guardian of law and order. According to M. Dansette, a large proportion of leading non-catholics like Cousin and Thiers now turned suddenly towards the Church, seeing in it an influence

[1] Ibid., p. 412.

capable of enforcing the obedience of the people. "There is not a Voltairian burdened with an income of a few thousand francs who is not anxious to send everybody to Mass, provided he doesn't have to go himself", said Ozanam in December 1849.[1]

The lay catholic leaders, Montalembert and Falloux, headed a "Party of Order", which supported the designs of Louis Napoleon, who skilfully represented himself as an ardent pro-catholic. They could congratulate themselves on having got *la loi Falloux* through Parliament in 1850, the law which at last granted the Church the right to establish its own secondary schools. The episcopate took the same line. Only one or two of the bishops, such as Cardinal de Bonald (1787–1870), Archbishop of Lyons, son of Viscount de Bonald, and Mgr Sibour (1792–1857), Archbishop of Paris, showed any awareness of the social problem. (Sibour, who succeeded Affre, was the second of three archbishops of Paris to die violent deaths within a period of twenty-five years.)

The French bishops knew little about socialism, but they did know the famous formula of Proudhon: "Property is robbery"; and they had a vague idea of the immoral implications of Fourier's teaching. Moreover, they were still haunted by the fear that the latest revolution, like that of 1789, would issue in a reign of terror.

Here, for example, is an extract from a pastoral letter of Mgr Clausel de Montals (1769–1857), Bishop of Chartres, dated 25 November 1848:

> They say that the Republic dates from Calvary, and the revolution is Christianity. No, Jesus Christ never mentioned political liberty in his discourses. The word "liberty" does not appear even once in the Gospel. Far from prescribing a form of government, he declared that his kingdom is not of this world. . . . Likewise when St Paul said, "My brethren, you are called to liberty", he meant liberty from the passions, not this unbridled liberty of the

[1] See Dansette, *Religious History of Modern France*, i, 265.

revolutionaries who, it seems, would like to see the terrible days of 1793 again, and who dare to say "property is robbery". . . .

What would become of France if she fell under the yoke of such rulers? But no! God will not allow her to be handed over defenceless and for ever to a horde of cannibals and to myriads of hangmen's assistants.[1]

The bishops failed to see the real causes of the Revolution. They attributed the spirit of insurrection to the subversive teaching of socialist leaders like Louis Blanc and to the dangerous ideas which they instilled into the popular mind. All that they could urge was a revival of catholic teaching and piety and private charity. Similarly, Louis Veuillot and *Univers*, after a brief flirtation with the idealism of the Revolution, became purely conservative and pumped into the minds of the clergy a horror of socialism.

As regards the Society of St Francis Xavier, which we saw had an important influence during the closing years of the July monarchy and which had to some extent brought together the social catholics of the right and left in practical activity, this also more or less petered out. For one thing, the February Revolution, by allowing liberty of association, opened the door to the formation of all sorts of clubs, and the Society of St Francis Xavier no longer profited from the circumstance that it could hold meetings in churches that would otherwise have been forbidden. Further, it had never given the workers any serious responsibility for its management, so that the more able and enterprising of them turned to the other societies that were now open to them. Again, the legitimists and the democrats fell out after the June insurrection, and the branches of the society went to pieces as a result of internal quarrels or of external suspicion.

The most considerable achievement of conservative social catholicism during the Second Republic was that of Armand de Melun and those associated with him. I have compared his rôle to that of Lord Shaftesbury in England, and we have seen that he

[2] See E. Sevrin, *Mgr Clausel de Montals* (1955), ii, 529.

had already done much work on proposals for social legislation and that in the last years of Louis Philippe was beginning to win the ear of the government. Although under the Second Republic he did not achieve all that he aimed at, he did get some valuable measures passed.

One of his first moves was to persuade the wives of the members of the provisional government to interest themselves in his society for the organization of charity and social relief, and in starting a "Fraternal Association in favour of the Poor". This arranged for the well-to-do to make themselves personally responsible for helping families that were destitute. The scheme had some good results, though it was only ephemeral. De Melun also persuaded the Society of St Vincent de Paul to extend its activities in this direction, and Archbishop Sibour too set up a charity organization society which provided for the relief of families in distress.

But de Melun's main object was to translate his social concern into legislation. If he used the word "charity" to cover the principles of his proposals, he did not mean charity in the traditional sense, but rather in using this word he hoped to remove the suspicions that the conservatives had of anything that smelt of socialism. He was emphatic that pauperism and destitution could be met only by State intervention, and that legislation should be preventive and not mere palliative. His proposals for the prevention of poverty included maternity-hospitals, day-nurseries, orphan asylums, popular education, vocational training, welfare associations for young working men, regulation of the hours of work, savings associations, and healthy housing. He would like to have seen a ministry of labour established in the government.

With a view to forwarding these aims, de Melun became a candidate for the National Assembly in May 1849 and was elected by a large majority. In the following month he persuaded the Assembly unanimously to appoint a committee of thirty members to study the question of public assistance for the poor. The committee was naturally mixed in its membership and the advocates of *laissez faire*, like Thiers, were strongly represented on it. Nevertheless, it produced a series of reports, and by persistent and resourceful negotiation de Melun managed to pass a body of social legislation through the National Assembly before the *coup d'état*. Laws were passed that dealt with unhealthy dwellings, with pension schemes, with mutual aid societies, with the education and guardianship of juvenile offenders, with hospitals, outdoor relief and medical services, and with the provision of baths. De Melun had just cause for self-congratulation. The social legislation of the Second Republic was a solid achievement, and for the most part it continued in force under the Second Empire and afterwards.

In May 1851 he was able to write:

> Already the working-men are singularly well disposed towards me, and boundlessly grateful for the good I have not yet done them. Saturday, one of the most advanced members of the Mountain [i.e. of the extreme left] . . . announced to me that in the day of the people's triumph only one member of the Right would not be excluded from the popular unity. It was I.[1]

The achievement of Armand de Melun, who was chiefly assisted in the National Assembly by his twin brother Anatole and by Arnaud de l'Ariège, is all the more remarkable when it is realized that the majority in the Assembly was haunted by the fear of socialism. In June 1850 Montalembert had laid it down in parliament: "There is no middle way—to-day it is necessary to choose between catholicism and socialism."[2] The conservative catholics of the Party of Order were dominated by this fear, though this does not mean that the views of all of them on the social problem were the same.

[1] Quoted by Moon, *The Labor Problem and the Social Catholic Movement in France*, p. 49, from the *Correspondant* (25 February 1882), p. 670.
[2] See Duroselle, *Revue d'Histoire de l'Église de France* (1948), p. 61.

Some, while much more cautious than de Melun, allowed that measures of social reform were needed, so long as they did not alter the social structure or modify the relations between capital and labour. Others held that private charity by itself was capable of meeting the situation and that no more than that was called for. This was the position of the *Univers* and of Montalembert. Most of them no doubt were indifferent to the social problem, and simply wanted to combat the menace of socialism by force and propaganda. But there was emerging at this time a new group of conservative catholics, who are to be reckoned as social catholics, since they developed their criticism of socialism into a positive, or at least a definite, social theory; the doctrine of the Counter-Revolution. This group was to become important under the Second Empire, and still more so after 1870: we shall consider it in due course.

Before we come to the *coup d'état* and its sequels, we may reflect that one reason why the social catholics were so small a minority in the Church of France was that, generally speaking, the clergy, formed under the July monarchy, had no direct knowledge of the industrial proletariat. The higher clergy were still recruited from the nobility or the *bourgeoisie* and, while most of the inferior clergy were of plebeian origin, they were usually of peasant stock and had been brought up in the country.

This ignorance of social facts made it possible for the clergy, and for catholics as a whole, to indulge the illusion (which has been common enough among Christians) that the cause of revolutionary movements and of social disturbance lies in the realm of theory or ideas, and that they are the result of the propagation of false teaching. Consequently, the grand way to counter them is by the dissemination and more active propagation of true teaching. So, for instance, we find Mgr René-François Regnier (1794–1881), Bishop of Angoulême, writing in a pastoral letter of February 1849:

It is in man's intelligence, dear brethren, it is in his faith and conscience that order essentially has its first cause and its guarantees. It is in fact ideas and doctrines that guide and control the moral world, and that create or quell revolutions.[1]

There was a failure to realize the truth, which Karl Marx was to exaggerate, that economic facts were more responsible for revolutionary movements than the ideas propagated by intellectuals, and that the impetus to socialism derived from the destitute conditions of the proletariat which could be remedied only by changes in the social structure. It was the virtue of the social catholics that they did have some understanding of this fact.

[1] See Duroselle, *Débuts*, pp. 417f.

3

France: The Second Empire

No one could be sure in advance what the effects of the *coup d'état* of December 1851 might be upon the fortunes of catholicism in France. Louis Napoleon, even if he had been trying to ingratiate himself with the catholics, had not hitherto shown much interest in the Church, and his ministers, so far as was known, were not likely to be either particularly favourable or particularly unfavourable to it. In point of fact, it seems that their attitude was purely opportunist. They wanted the support of as many elements in the nation as possible, and to show at least apparent favour to the Church should have the effect of reconciling legitimists to the new régime.

There were certainly catholics who for their part were hopeful at the outset that the Prince-President would give the Church what it had long been asking for. So, directly after the *coup d'état* we find Montalembert requesting Louis Napoleon to abolish the Organic Articles of 1802, against which the papacy had always protested because of their gallican character, and to grant complete liberty of education. He also suggested a reconstitution of the pre-revolutionary corporations. So he said to the Prince:

You know what your uncle said . . .: "In the long run, the sword is conquered by the spirit." That being so, on what spirit are you going to rely for support? The rationalist spirit which flourishes in the University is plainly hostile to you: your *coup d'état* has profoundly shocked it. The catholic spirit is your only possible auxiliary.[1]

Louis Veuillot was equally sanguine. On 20 December 1851 he wrote:

> Bonaparte has saved us. His intentions with regard to the Church are excellent. We now have good grounds for hoping to obtain liberties which we should hardly have dreamed of a month ago. . . . Bonaparte is religious and even superstitious rather than Christian . . .[2]

And a little later:

> The ministers are unbelievers of a quite new type: neither *philosophes* nor voltairians, and intelligent enough to see, first, that the Church is a great political force and, secondly, that this force must remain free.[3]

Some of the new government's early actions seemed to encourage these hopes, though Montalembert, who might have had most influence with Louis Napoleon, soon broke with him because of the confiscation of the property of the House of Orleans and other blatantly illiberal measures. Among the steps that were taken to woo, or to seduce, the catholics were the giving of seats in the Senate to the French cardinals, easier arrangements for the authorization of religious communities for women, the appointment of more chaplains to government institutions, and the assignment of 5,000,000 francs from the property of the House of Orleans for the poorest clergy.

Such measures proved sufficient to attract catholic support. Legitimist bishops, like Clausel de Montals of Chartres, who was a gallican, and Pie of Poitiers, who was an ultramontane, welcomed the dictatorship of Louis Napoleon with enthusiasm,

---

[1] See Lecanuet, *Montalembert*, iii, 44.
[2] See Jean Maurain, *La politique ecclésiastique du Second Empire* (1930), p. 15.
[3] See Sevrin, *Mgr Clausel de Montals*, ii, 648.

reckoning that the return to an authoritarian régime would prepare the way for the restoration of the Bourbons.

Already in 1849, when Louis Napoleon had visited Chartres to open the railway to Paris, the bishop had addressed him in flattering terms.[1] In June 1851 he had had an interview with the Prince-President in which he had tried to point out to him his true mission, namely to follow the glorious example of General Monk at the time of the restoration of Charles II. Both these bishops believed in the sincerity of Louis Napoleon's religious sentiments, Pie having been impressed by the fact that he had seen him make the sign of the cross at the beginning of a sermon when other people did not.[2] Happy statesmen who can so easily captivate the prelates of Christ's Church!

At the time of the plebiscite, when Louis Napoleon was voted absolute powers, the Bishop of Chartres issued a directive to his clergy that they should vote affirmatively. This directive, coming as it did from a well-known legitimist, received nation-wide publicity and had a considerable influence on the catholic vote.[3] In fact, Sibour of Paris and Dupanloup, now Bishop of Orleans, seem to have been the only bishops who did not take this line, and Sibour rallied to the new régime subsequently.

Despite the catholic support which it thus received, the new régime made no fundamental changes in the interests of the Church. The government wanted to encourage the Church only as a counterforce to revolutionary and socialist propaganda. When therefore the government abolished all civil liberties, it maintained the Church's existing liberties and made a few further insubstantial concessions to it. The catholics almost unanimously welcomed the destruction of civil liberties and, except for the little group of liberal catholics, accepted enthusiastically the authoritarianism of the new régime.

Veuillot expressed the general mind of the Church, or at least of the clergy, when he said on 8 January 1852: "As regards

[1] Ibid., ii, 537. [2] Ibid., ii, 636f. [3] Ibid., ii, 645.

liberty, we ask liberty for the Church, that is, liberty for what is good ... We no longer consider, as we used to do till 1848, that liberty for good necessarily involves liberty for what is bad. .... Let what is good be free, but not what is bad: that is how we understand liberty"[1] (i.e they had turned their backs on their previous demand for liberty for all, and now wanted it only for themselves).

Pope Pius IX joined in the general applause, congratulating the French Ambassador to the Holy See on the authoritarianism of the new régime. The Church's solidarity with the dictatorship, and its reversion from its recent flirtation with the spirit of democracy, were to cause bitter and permanent hostility and distrust in all French liberals and republicans, the legacy of which remains unto this day. But what concerns us here is that these circumstances go far to explain what happened to social catholicism under the Second Empire.

The Church's identification of itself with the dictatorship of Napoleon III sufficiently accounts for the fact that the *coup d'état* marks the virtual disappearance of the social catholicism of the left. It would not reappear for a long time. Republicanism and social democracy were at one fell swoop destroyed or at least driven underground. It is true that in the later, liberalizing period of the Second Empire the non-Christian democrats were able to lift up their heads again and to prepare themselves for the opportunities that would come to them in 1870. But the Christian democrats of 1848–51 were too weak to revive their forces. There were only a few stray manifestations of their existence during the Empire, and there is no clear line of continuity between them and the Christian democrats who emerged towards the end of the century. Maret, who had been the ablest theologian among the Christian democrats, eventually rallied to the Empire, and became one of its most trusted advisers in

[1] See Louis Veuillot, *Œuvres complètes* (1934), xxxi, 17.

ecclesiastical affairs. While there is nothing to show that he changed his social views, he was henceforth absorbed in his academic work as dean of the faculty of theology at the Sorbonne, and in his courageous endeavour to uphold the cause of liberal catholicism against Veuillot and the ultramontanes. The story of social catholicism during the Empire is then that of its right or conservative wing.

The advent of Louis Napoleon in some ways made the prospects of the conservative social catholics brighter. In the first place, it was his policy, as we have said, to win the support of the Church and to give the catholics scope, so long as they were prepared to pay the necessary price in supporting the régime, and this the conservatives were happy enough to do.

Secondly, it must be borne in mind that the Napoleonic idea of government was always double-faced: authoritarian and anti-revolutionary on the one hand, and reforming and paternalistic on the other. "Do not reproach Napoleon I for his dictatorship", Louis Napoleon had written. "It brought us liberty as the ploughshare that digs the furrow prepares the fertility of the fields."[1] Napoleon III followed his uncle in this respect, and was *homo duplex*. Thus it could be expected that the conservative social catholics, though few of them were bonapartists by prior conviction, would find that their attitude to the social problem was close enough to that of the Emperor to make it possible for them to do the kind of things they wanted to do, for their standpoint too was basically paternalistic.

Thirdly, Louis Napoleon had already shown an interest in the cause of the workers. In 1844 he had published a book on the *Extinction of Pauperism*. Doubtless, the motive of his interest was not purely philanthropic. He sought the support of the workers, as of the Church, for his dictatorial designs. But it was to the good that he was actively interested in the needs and welfare of the working class, in a way that Louis Philippe had never been.

[1] See G. Duveau, *La vie ouvrière en France sous le Second Empire* (1946), p. 47.

The *coup d'état* could not have been carried through, nor could the Empire have been established, without the goodwill of the workers who like the catholics hoped that their aspirations were going to be met.

The two sides of the double-faced character of Louis Napoleon's strategy with regard to the workers was shown at once in his ruthless suppression of all socialist opposition, on the one hand, and in the measures he adopted to improve the condition of the working class, on the other. These included not only measures of social reform, such as welfare institutions and boards of conciliation, but also the great increase of industrial enterprise and the vast programme of public works—the rebuilding of Paris, above all—which issued in a wave of prosperity from which the workers benefited to a very considerable extent, while the capitalists were of course making their fortunes.[1]

In at least one of Napoleon's social reforms—the encouragement of friendly societies—the conservative social catholics, Armand de Melun in particular, played a significant part. He and his friends had for some time been recommending friendly societies as a means of enabling the workers to meet the hazards of the industrial system.

De Melun was a legitimist, not a bonapartist, though not so fanatical a legitimist as his wife, who apparently after his death destroyed the correspondence that her husband had had at this time with "the usurper"! De Melun, in view of his antecedents, was taken aback when he was invited to dine with the Prince-President on 17 March 1852. He thought at first that the Prince's secretary must have made a mistake, till he learned that it was Archbishop Sibour who, when he found that the Prince wanted to do something about friendly societies, had advised him to consult de Melun.

The archbishop was also present at the dinner. After the meal,

[1] See Duveau, op. cit., for an exhaustive study of the conditions of the workers under the Second Empire.

they retired to the Prince's study and de Melun in his *Mémoires* gives this account of what transpired. The Prince

> began by saying how necessary it was to do something in the interests of the people. . . . There was one institution that seemed to him to meet, better than any other, the conditions of the problem that had to be solved: the *Friendly Society* which was both practical and popular . . . He insisted much on the advantage of uniting in this work the different social classes, through admitting the well-to-do as honorary members, and the workers as participating members. He had therefore decided to favour with all his power the propagation and development of so useful an institution, which was recommended by policy as well as by beneficence, and he had called us together to consult us about the best means of introducing, even into the smallest village, the spirit and practice of mutual insurance. [1]

It became apparent that the Prince and his ministers contemplated issuing a government decree that a friendly society was to be started in every commune under the presidency of the mayor, and that all proprietors and workers were to be compelled to join as honorary and participating members respectively. De Melun vigorously protested against a compulsory system which, in his view, savoured of State socialism. He urged instead that a scheme of approved, voluntary friendly societies should be adopted. The Prince listened attentively, chain-smoking the while, and at 11 p.m. dismissed his guests in order to go to the opera.

The next day, de Melun was summoned to meet the President of the Council, Rouher, who asked him to take the proposal in hand. De Melun said that he would not touch it unless it were a voluntary scheme, and he got his way. He prepared both the decree and the explanation of it that was published in the *Moniteur*. The decree provided that in every commune, where there was need for it, a friendly society could be established by

[1] See Duroselle, *Débuts*, p. 502.

the prefect with the help of the mayor and the parish priest. Those societies, which were formally approved by the government, would have certain financial advantages and their presidents would be nominated by the Prince-President himself. Other societies would be authorized, that is, given a permit, but they would not have the same privileges as the approved societies. A central commission was set up under the government to superintend the operation of the scheme, and de Melun was one of its principal members.

These friendly societies, many of which had been in existence previously, had a considerable success during the Second Empire, and they showed a steady growth. By 1869 there were over 6,000 societies, approved or authorized, with over 900,000 members, of whom about one-eighth were honorary members (members who subscribed without themselves claiming benefits). The societies made payments in case of sickness or injury, and paid funeral expenses, but did not provide unemployment benefits.

The friendly societies were of four types: those for members of a single trade or profession; those that were multi-professional for members who lived in the same area, for example, a town, a parish, or a quarter of a city; municipal societies, started by the mayor and parish priest for a commune; societies founded by employers for their employees. De Melun preferred the second type. Many of the societies had a more or less religious character; they had at least an annual festival in church, and some were specifically catholic, following the pattern of the Society of St Francis Xavier before 1848.

In Paris and the surrounding area there were about twenty catholic friendly societies, embracing 6,000 to 7,000 members. But that is not a large number in regard to the number of workers. By and large, it would seem that it was artisans who belonged to them, not factory hands or labourers. The paternalistic and patronizing character of the catholic societies was especially objectionable to the more enterprising and self-respecting workers. They appealed rather to the docile and to the devout, which has perhaps been too common a characteristic of Christian institutions, not only in France.

This appears to have been the case too with the other good works to which the social catholics applied themselves at this time. The work of the Society of St Vincent de Paul among young people continued, and indeed increased. About 1860 there were approximately 1,300 "conferences" in existence, which probably indicated a total membership of between 30,000 and 40,000—not 100,000 as some books say.[1] But in 1860 the relations between the Church and the imperial government were seriously deteriorating, and this circumstance had an inevitable effect on social catholic activities.

Napoleon III's refusal to maintain his defence of the temporal power of the pope alienated most of the influential catholics in France, and especially Louis Veuillot who had hitherto exalted the Emperor to the position of a new Charlemagne or St Louis. Veuillot now violently attacked him because of his betrayal of the papacy. The imperial government was naturally offended by this show of ingratitude for all the favour it considered it had shown to the Church in France. Moreover, it had never intended to abandon the traditional gallicanism of all French governments, and therefore it was alarmed by the rapid spread of ultramontanism and clericalism in the Church and by the theocratic pretensions that were constantly voiced by the *Univers*. For these reasons the Government decided on a policy which, while still intended to be favourable to religion, aimed at arresting the encroachments of papal authority in France. A further cause of its viewing catholic organizations with suspicion was of course the fact that legitimism was still rife among them.

So we find Napoleon's minister, Rouland, in a long memorandum which he prepared in April 1860 on the policy to be pursued with regard to the Church, saying among other things

[1] Ibid., p. 550.

that the government should concern itself with the large lay associations that were really under the control of the clergy and the legitimist party. This advice was taken, and catholic societies, even where their professed objects were purely religious or philanthropic, soon found themselves being harassed.

In particular, the Society of St Vincent de Paul was attacked. In 1861 the government asked for a confidential report from the prefects about the activities of this society in their departments. It appeared that the legitimists were often in a majority in the conferences (branches) of the society, many of which had not sought the legal recognition which the law required. Moreover, its hierarchial organization, with provincial councils and a general council in Paris, together with its international associations and its contacts with Rome, seemed to make it a potentially dangerous anti-government force. The government therefore decreed that the general council of the society should be dissolved, and that all local conferences must secure legal recognition.

About 400 conferences, namely those that were dominated by legitimists, preferred to go into voluntary dissolution rather than seek legal authorization, and elsewhere the society was greatly weakened by the defection of members who either did not want to be mixed up with a suspect organization or objected to making any concession to the imperial requirements.[1] An attempt to defend the Society of St Vincent de Paul in the Senate was made by its friends there, including two cardinals. They asserted that the society was purely charitable and that it could not be politically dangerous, because it was under the supervision of the episcopate, because it had many bonapartists among its members, and because there was nothing secret in its organization. The general council and the provincial councils, so far from inciting the conferences to go beyond their charitable objects, had censured any that had let themselves become involved in political action. If they had not sought government authorization,

[1] For this whole story, see Maurain, op. cit., pp. 554-67.

that had been with a view to preserving the society's political neutrality. The cardinal protector of the society, through whom, according to the government, Rome directed it, had in the course of nine years received only eleven letters from Rome of which he had left eight unanswered! But this defence had no effect.

The social catholics were also active in a variety of guilds and clubs for apprentices or for young convalescents, but these too seem to have reached only members of the artisan class, not the factory workers.[1] While most of the catholic organizations were designed to win or keep young people to religious observance and to bring them together for purposes of recreation, some were concerned with their working conditions and with safeguarding them from exploitation and ill-treatment. These catholic organizations, usually and significantly known as "patronages" (a word that cannot be satisfactorily translated), were under clerical control, and with rare exceptions little or no responsibility was allowed to the young workers themselves.

There was, for example, a priest at Marseilles named Joseph Timon-David (b. 1823) who devoted himself to the service of young workers. While at the seminary of St Sulpice in Paris, he had met Ledreuille of the Society of St Francis Xavier and had been fired with a desire to imitate his example, but he had a much narrower conception than Ledreuille of how to serve the workers. "What we call Youth Work", he said, "is a pious association of children and young people, belonging to the working classes, who in their spare time meet together in order to play innocent games and to sanctify their souls by the practices of Christian devotion."[2]

Timon-David was a political reactionary. He had been anti-republican even in 1848, and all his life was strongly opposed to liberal catholicism. His object was to build up small groups of young workers in an intense spirituality. It was essential that they

[1] See Duroselle, p. 566.   [2] Ibid., pp. 563f.

should all be under the control of the clergy. He was opposed to any sort of lay leadership in this sphere, and went so far as to assert that liberty of education in France had been won by the bishops, not by laymen, thus denying the part that had been played by Montalembert, Falloux, and others. His methods were thoroughly pietistic. He was so attached to his own methods that he was contemptuous of other attempts to serve young workers on a broader basis.

A much more genuine type of social catholic was Maurice Maignen (b. 1822), who was a layman. As a young man he had for a time lost his faith. It was the influence of socialist writers, especially fourierists, together with the Society of St Vincent de Paul, that had won him to the service of young workers. The enterprises, for which he was responsible, especially the circles of catholic workers, were more broadly based and more imaginative. He saw the need to give responsibility for leadership to the workers themselves. He encouraged the arrangement of frequent exhibitions at which young workers and apprentices exhibited the products of their craftsmanship. He opened a settlement in Paris, a large house in the Boulevard Montparnasse, where there was a fine garden at the disposal of young workers. He also started a flourishing consumers' co-operative society for them. He sought to emulate the much larger companionship for young catholic workers that had been established in Germany (see chapter 5). But in France at this time Maignen's effort was almost unique. It shows, however, what might have been done on a much larger scale if there had been more leaders of this stamp.

But of the catholics as a whole, including the social catholics, it must be said that they were in their way just as paternalistic as the imperial government. Their conservatism made them suspicious of any tendency that gave power to the working classes, especially to trade unions. The consequence was that the workers' movements, which developed in the later years of the Empire, were not only quite detached from Christian influences but were more or less anti-clerical. The Church was reaping the results of its rash surrender to the seductions of Louis Napoleon after the *coup d'état* and of its identification with the imperial authoritarianism.

Nevertheless, from 1860 de Melun and the Society of Charitable Economy, for which he was responsible, with its journal *Annales de la Charité*, became much larger in outlook and more interested in the needs of the workers as such, not only of paupers, and also in social remedies rather than in bringing relief to individuals. This enlargement of outlook was partly due to participation in the international conferences and congresses which were held in different countries at this period for people who were concerned with industrial progress and social welfare.

For instance, a meeting of the Congrès International de Bienfaisance, which had been founded in 1857, was held in London in June 1862, concurrently with the annual meeting of the (English) National Association for the Promotion of Social Science. Lord Brougham presided over the latter, and Lord Shaftesbury over the former. At this Congress de Melun gave a long report on "Charity in France". I reproduce here the summary of his speech which appeared in *The Times* newspaper (11 June 1862), since it gives a concise account of the welfare measures that were now in operation in France, for many of which the conservative social catholics could take a substantial share of credit.

M. le Vicomte A. de Melun gave a very full and detailed account of the charities of France, of which he enumerated such a multitude that if only a half of them do their work efficiently there must be few forms of social misery in the length and breadth of the land for which relief in some shape or other has not been provided. Extensive provision is made for the children of the poor in the shape of public nurseries and schools. By the law of 1833 the communes are bound to maintain free schools at their own charge, the State merely contributing to the cost of their first establishment. The reformatory schools of France on the principle of Mettray have acquired a high reputation. Savings-banks, provident clubs, hospitals for the infirm of mind and body, asylums for infants and aged persons, and societies for the publication of edifying literature, are, of course, common to most European countries. Among the benevolent institutions peculiar to France are the agricultural colonies, which are 36 in number, and are intended to counteract the drain of the population into the large towns, and to qualify the members for rural labours. There is also a system of "patronage", under which youths are apprenticed on leaving school, and kept under a kindly supervision until they arrive at man's estate. The question of house accommodation for the lower classes is just now as perplexing in Paris as in London. The renovation of the French capital which has substituted magnificent mansions for the wretched and unwholesome dens which formerly existed, has rescued the poor from the filth and squalor of their old abodes, only to leave them with scarcely any shelter at all. Attempts have been made to establish towns of operatives; but without success, except in one case of one or two centres of industry, such as Mulhouse. It is satisfactory to learn that France is beginning to appreciate sanitary measures. Since 1850 there has been a commission to enforce such repairs or improvements in the dwellings of the poor as may be required to render them healthy. In regard to foundling hospitals, M. de Melun mentioned that when the Government abolished the *tours*, or apertures in the wall, through which a child could be delivered without exposing the mother to recognition, the number of foundlings was diminished, but the cases of infanticide increased, while the amount of illegitimacy remained about the same as before. The extensive interference of the State in the charitable and philanthropic institutions of France was a very striking feature of the report.

An incidental remark by the Comte de Melun that all the evil in the world had sprung from liberty drew a spirited response from M. Walewski, a member of the Institut, who traced all the blessings of humanity to the same source. The Comte, however, explained that all he meant was that evil existed in the world because God had given man the freedom of choice between good and evil in his acts.

Two days later *The Times* contained a description of the *cité ouvrière* of Mulhouse, which had been given at a later session of the Congress. At the final session there was a heated discussion between the French-speaking delegates about the merits of compulsory education. De Melun and the other catholic delegates said that they were against it.

It does not seem to have occurred to the conservative social catholics that the working classes ought to be educated in order that they might be better qualified to fight their own battles and to improve their own conditions. They were paternalists who believed in doing things for the workers, but not in enabling the workers to do things for themselves.

Mention may be made at this point of a remarkable document that has lately come to light.[1] It is a project for a mission to the workers of Paris, which appears to have been drafted in 1855 and to have been submitted to Archbishop Sibour who had discussed it with his clergy before his assassination on 3 January 1857. Perhaps it was his death that prevented the project from materializing. It was a well-conceived plan for an association of secular priests who would freely give part of their time—say, one day a week—to meeting, teaching, and addressing the workers of Paris. The document was probably produced by Abbé Ledreuille. It looks like an interesting anticipation of the idea of the Mission de Paris.[2]

We must now turn to a consideration of catholic social philosophy under the Empire. The most important development here was the elaboration of the theory of the Counter-Revolution, notably by Frédéric Le Play (1806–82). He wielded a very extensive influence, after his death as well as during his lifetime. For instance, at the time of the great dock strike in England in

[1] See *Archives de Sociologie des Religions*, No. 6 (July–December 1958), pp. 36–46.

[2] Cp. Émile Poulat, *Journal d'un prêtre d'après-demain* (1961), introduction.

1889 Cardinal Manning said: "Whatever I may have done in this matter has been due to the counsels and teaching of my illustrious master, Le Play."[1]

Le Play[2] was born in a fishing village near Honfleur. His earliest recollections were of the sufferings of the fishing community at the hands of the British fleet which was maintaining a blockade of the coast. His father died while he was still a child. Almost as soon as he could get about he went foraging with other children for the bare necessities of existence. This early experience impressed upon him that the wealth of a family is measured not by money but by its collective resources in food, firewood, etc. Had the Norman fisher folk depended at that time on cash earnings, most of them must have perished.

After this initial experience, Le Play was taken off to Paris by a wealthy uncle and aunt, and given the beginnings of an education which took him finally to the École Polytechnique, where he passed out with distinction. The earlier part of his professional career was spent as a mining engineer, and he made notable contributions to the growth of the French mining industry. In connection with his researches he visited mining centres in North Germany and elsewhere, and it was in the course of these expeditions that his interest in social science or sociology took shape. He was interested not only in mines but in miners, and when he had collected information about engineering methods he went on to study the manner of life of families engaged in industry. At length he became so absorbed in these sociological inquiries and studies that he decided to devote the rest of his life to them and to the propagation of his beliefs about the right lines of social reform.

[1] Manning was the lonely pioneer of social catholicism in England, see G. P. McEntee, *The Social Catholic Movement in Great Britain* (New York, 1927); V. A. McClelland, *Cardinal Manning* (1962), ch. v.

[2] On Le Play, see Dorothy Herbertson, *The Life of Frédéric Le Play* (1950); Roger Grand (ed.), *Recueil d'études sociales à la mémoire de Frédéric Le Play* (1956); Duroselle, pp. 672–84.

He believed that he had discovered the importance, for the understanding of social life and institutions, of the *inductive* method that was employed in the natural sciences. Human nature, as well as nature, should be studied empirically. He had no use for projects for social reform that were based on theoretical considerations or on general principles such as liberty, fraternity, and equality—the "false dogmas of '89", as he called them. Instead, he set himself to find out, through a close observation of how men actually lived, what were the deep-seated, underlying causes of social well-being and of social disease. Doctrinaire reforms that might look well on paper were prone to create worse evils than those they sought to remedy.

In 1855 he published the first edition of *Les Ouvriers Européens*. This was a series of monographs, each of which was a study of a different working-class family, including a detailed analysis of its budget of receipts and expenditure. The families selected for study were of various nationality and background. This piece of sociological field-work, which was the outcome of twenty-five years of travel and investigation, made such an impression that a society, known as the Society for Social Economy, was founded in 1856 for the further prosecution of Le Play's methods. There are still those who regard him as the father—or at least as a father—of social science as an empirical discipline. Others, however, consider that his claim to be purely inductive in his methods was vitiated by the fact that he interpreted—and indeed looked for—the data he collected and classified on the basis of quite definite and limiting presuppositions.

"Populations", according to Le Play, "consist not of individuals but of families. The task of observation would be vague, indefinite and inconclusive, if in every locality it were required to extend to individuals differing in age and sex. It becomes precise, definite and conclusive when its object is the family." This preoccupation with the family as the fundamental social reality was the strength of Le Play's system, though it may also have been its limitation. It does seem that he had more of a one-track mind than is becoming in a professed empiricist. However that may be, he distinguished three types of family.

First, the patriarchal family, the type characteristic of pastoral peoples, which is exceedingly stable but unprogressive. The father is the chief administrator of all family affairs, and at his death all goods pass to the eldest son.

Secondly, what he called the stock family or the family group, which is both conservative and progressive. Children and grand-children no longer remain under paternal authority throughout life. With a single exception they leave the family hearth and proceed to found new homes. The chosen heir becomes the new head of the family by paternal wish, not of legal right. The property thus passes to the worthiest, who is thought best able to preserve it.

Thirdly, there is the unstable family, where all the children, so soon as they arrive at maturity, quit the home and set up for themselves. At the father's death, the family, which is already scattered, is completely dissolved. The patrimony is equally divided between all the members. This is the régime born of individualism, which is characteristic of modern societies, especially of France. The family loses every trace of solidarity.

Le Play's sympathy was entirely with the second type of family—the family group which holds the balance between the spirit of conservatism and the spirit of innovation. A father's authority over his children is the indispensable element in the stability of society, and he must be armed with the right to disinherit, if necessary. He is responsible for the support of his family and for its moral and religious training.

This conception of paternal authority and responsibility Le Play regarded as the key to a wholesome social order. In an industrial society every business and factory should be seen, so far as possible, as a family. A master's authority over his men was analogous to that of a father over his children. The relations between employer and worker should be defined by custom and should normally be permanent. There should be social contacts and co-operation between them outside, as well as inside, the factory. This was known as the system of *patronage*. It was contrasted with employment merely on a cash basis, where men are taken on for a temporary job and turned adrift when it is completed. In that case the master feels no interest in them. They come he knows not whence to go he knows not whither.

In Le Play's view, a man who is operating a large business for his own profit or loss is in every way preferable to the representative of an impersonal company. He was opposed to large organizations, where personal contact and responsibility are at a minimum, and still more to government interference. Le Play obviously pinned his faith to the benevolence of employers. The salvation of the working classes could come only from above, through *patronage*. He had no use for workers' associations or for trade unions. But it is a fair question whether this paternalistic theory of social salvation has not been refuted by repeated empirical observations. This is what John Stuart Mill said about it:

> No times can be pointed out in which the higher classes of this or any other country performed a part even distantly resembling the one assigned to them in this theory. It is an idealization, grounded on the conduct and character of here and there an individual. All privileged and powerful classes, as such, have used their power in the interest of their own selfishness . . . I do not affirm that what has always been must always be . . . This, at least, seems to me undeniable, that long before the superior classes could be sufficiently improved to govern in the tutelary manner supposed, the inferior classes would be too much improved to be so governed. [1]

Le Play's version of catholic social doctrine, which was based on religion, property, the family, and *patronage*, appealed chiefly to capitalists, or at least to the upper and middle classes, and it geared in with the monarchist and aristocratic ideas that were

[1] J. S. Mill, *Principles of Political Economy* (7th ed. 1871), ii, 335.

congenial to the leaders of French catholicism. His belief in the natural propensity of man to evil, which led to his laying great emphasis on the rôle of religion in inculcating obedience to the moral law, was also naturally congenial to the catholics. Further, the fact that his theories were put forth with a vast array of impressive evidence, scientifically presented, gave the conservative catholics the gratifying confidence that, in subscribing to the thesis of the Counter-Revolution, they were not being obscurantist or reactionary, but that they had a true system with which to rebut democratic and socialistic movements.

Similar ideas were propounded by Charles Périn (1815–1905),[1] a catholic professor of the University of Louvain, though for him the social problem was one more of morals than of institutions. If everybody would be charitable and industrious, the social problem would disappear. Périn was reactionary and monarchist in politics, but at bottom he was a liberal in economic theory and stood for *laissez faire*. So he said:

> As soon as you admit that the State has the right of regulation in questions of production, as soon as you accept, as the basis of economic organization, the intervention of the State in the relations between private interests, you are heading straight toward socialism.[2]

Périn advocated the formation of guilds which would bring together employers and working men, and in which the virtues of duty, renunciation, and charity would be cultivated. All that was positive in his system was paternalistic. It presupposed the maintenance of the social hierarchy and a precarious confidence in the beneficence of the upper classes.

Le Play and Périn—and also Émile Keller, another theoretician of the Counter-Revolution, whom we shall be meeting in

---

[1] On Périn, see Duroselle, pp. 697f.; Moon, op. cit., pp. 58–68; M. Becqué, *Le Cardinal Dechamps* (1956), ii, 281–313.

[2] See Moon, op. cit., p. 63.

chapter 7—had numerous followers who sought to popularize their ideas. A number of writers, for instance, produced histories of the charitable activities of the Church in times ancient and modern, and extolled the institutions of the *ancien régime*. There was also quite an amount of literature which aimed at addressing the workers themselves, though with doubtful success.

There was a weekly paper called *L'Ouvrier*, founded in 1861. Its manifesto in the opening number said:

> We are not concerned with politics. The worker needs something else. Instead of crying out against the pope and the priests, Gentlemen of the Press, deign to have a look at the class that suffers. . . How many questions there are on which light needs to be thrown: competition, wages, unemployment, sanitary conditions, morals, religion, homes for the aged, etc. Our aim, comrades, is to study all these questions.[1]

It went on to say that its columns were open to every intelligent and experienced worker who was disposed to communicate to others his ideas for improving the condition of the working class. But, in point of fact, only a few articles were concerned with social questions. The paper's character was more or less what in England we associate with parish magazines. It does, however, seem to have had a certain vogue, and was reckoned to have 150,000 to 200,000 readers weekly.

The theme of the Counter-Revolution was taken up by the bishops and other clergy. Typical of episcopal utterances are these words of Mgr Louis-Charles Féron (1793–1879), Bishop of Clermont:

> To claim to be able to do away with poverty is utopian. The working classes constitute the mass of the population in all countries. They cannot fail to produce a very large number of these casualties of the social order who are called the poor. If you took away the riches of the wealthy, you would not provide any general relief even for a single day.[2]

---

[1] See Duroselle, p. 687.   [2] Ibid., p. 689.

Another bishop declared that works of charity were one of the essential marks of the Church. In contrast to those mad doctrines that would make society responsible for the merciful severity which is maintained in this world by the divine justice and goodness, the Church had never preached to the people the total destruction of suffering. Even Mgr Georges Darboy (1813–71), the liberal-minded Archbishop of Paris, who had welcomed the February Revolution with enthusiasm and shown socialistic sympathies, fell into line and made his own the epigram: "Nations die of hunger only when they are already dead in vice."[1]

As we come to the year 1870, we arrive at the melancholy conclusion that, as regards the social problems that were consequent upon the Industrial Revolution, French catholicism was back in about the same position as it had been forty or fifty years before. Throughout the period the great majority of catholics had been indifferent to the problems, through a failure to comprehend what they were. But the enterprises—whether theoretical or practical—of those who may properly be called social catholics appeared to have had no lasting effect. The only positive thing that those catholics, who were concerned about the condition of the industrial poor, had to recommend was almsgiving and works of charity.

The reasons for the fruitlessness of the manifestations of social catholicism, which we have so far been considering, are no doubt complicated. The social catholics of the left were too utopian and doctrinaire; those of the right too fearful of the bugbears of socialism and democracy, and not fearful enough of the corrupting effects of power and privilege. Beyond that, the Church for which they sought to speak and act was for the most part indifferent to their concerns. With rare exceptions its hierarchy was incapable of reading the signs of the times and was without

[1] Ibid., pp. 691f.

any sense of the prophetic office of the Church. But even if French catholics had at this time been more aware of social realities, it must be allowed that the political fluctuations and upheavals of the period, and finally the restrictions imposed on all independent action under the Second Empire, would have been highly adverse to any well-conceived policy of social reconstruction.

4

Belgium: 1830-70

Belgium[1] is a small country but it has played a very important part in the history of Europe. At the time of the Reformation it was one of the areas where catholic resistance to protestantism was strongest. In the seventeenth century jansenism originated in the University of Louvain. From a military point of view, the European powers have always had a natural interest in a region where three great navigable rivers converge, and where there are ports of vast economic and commercial value. Though the country's resources are rich, over-population has produced recurring economic crises.

When Napoleon I fell and the statesmen of Europe set about fabricating a new order, the Belgian provinces were assigned to William I, the protestant King of Holland, but the Belgian people, especially the catholics, bitterly resented the dominance of their northern neighbour. In 1830 they succeeded in achieving their independence as a result of a united effort on the part of the catholics and the liberals who elsewhere in Europe were ranged in hostile camps. For a considerable period after 1830 the catholics and the liberals continued to work together on a basis of what was called "unionism".

[1] For Belgium, see above all Rudolf Rezsohazy, *Origines et formation du catholicisme social en Belgique, 1842–1909* (Louvain, 1958); also Henri Haag, *Les origines du catholicisme libéral en Belgique, 1789–1839* (Louvain, 1950); A. Simon, *L'Église catholique et les débuts de la Belgique indépendante* (Wetteren, 1949); Maurice Vaussard, *Histoire de la démocratie chrétienne: France, Belgique, Italie* (Paris, 1956).

This combination of catholicism with liberalism in Belgium was possible for various reasons. The catholic leaders had been much influenced by the liberal catholicism of Lamennais, and the influence had not been in one direction only, for Lamennais had argued from the collaboration in Belgium that the same should be possible in France. Again, the experience which the Belgian catholics had had of subjection to the civil government of the protestant King of Holland, who had tried to use his royal authority so as to control the Church, had prepared them to welcome the separation of Church and State and the constitutional liberties of which catholics in other countries were still for the most part fearful. On the other hand, the Belgian liberals, unlike those in France, were mostly practising catholics. Their liberalism might be anti-clerical, but it was not anti-catholic. On both sides therefore there were factors at work that made collaboration possible. Liberal catholicism became popular in Belgium while it was still regarded as anathema elsewhere.

However, as was the case in France, the liberal catholics were not necessarily any more alive to the social questions consequent upon industrialization than the conservatives were. There were in fact greater obstacles in the way of the development of a social catholicism in Belgium than there were elsewhere. So far from there being a natural connection between liberal catholicism and social catholicism, they were often antithetic. For the liberalism of the liberal catholics disposed them to believe in economic liberalism or *laissez faire*, and to be hostile to government legislation that interfered with the free working of the industrial system.

There were other factors too that retarded the development of social catholicism in Belgium. Culturally, it was a backward country, in which the new forces that had been generated by the French Revolution had had little effect, and the same is true of the romantic movement. It is a Belgian historian, Henri Pirenne, who has described the condition of his compatriots before 1830 as follows:

> Illiteracy abounded. The *bourgeoisie* read nothing but the news-papers. The clergy had only a seminary training, and knew only enough Latin to say mass. The aristocracy disclaimed all intellectual curiosity. Nowhere was there any taste for serious study. There were no public or private libraries . . .[1]

Even those catholics, who had some political standing and enterprise, belonged culturally to the *ancien régime*. So we find, for instance, Louis de Robiano (1781-1855), who was an author and a Member of Parliament, taking the trouble to write a tract[2] addressed to ladies and young people of quality, urging them not to travel by coach where they would run the risk of consorting with common people, such as notaries, lawyers, and industrialists! What these aristocrats thought of the peasants and the dwellers in the slums can be imagined. The wretched condition of the victims of industrialism was viewed without comprehension or sympathy: it was taken to be in the nature of things.

And the condition of the proletariat was worse in Belgium than it was in France or England. The capitalists had an entirely free hand, and legislation was all on their side. The workers were illiterate and demoralized, incapable of taking any steps to defend their interests even if the law had permitted them to do so. Their wages were pitiful and tended to decrease throughout the first half of the century, and their employment, such as it was, was hopelessly insecure. In 1848—which, it is true, was a particularly bad year—there were nearly a million unemployed indigents. In the following year an epidemic of typhus and cholera resulted in over 22,000 deaths.[3] Housing conditions were ghastly.

When employment was available, the worker had to work for

---

[1] See Vaussard, op. cit., pp. 136f.   [2] Ibid., p. 137.
[3] See Rezsohazy, op. cit., pp. 2f.

anything up to fifteen hours a day. In the factories and workshops no consideration was given to the workers' health, nor had they adequate protection against the dangers to which machinery exposed them. The employers used the labour of women and children wherever they could, since it was cheaper. For example, in 1840 of 10,701 workers employed in the coalmines in the province of Liège, 1,690 were children.

The Church showed no awareness of the situation in which it was set, and in the rare instances where the bishops paid any attention to it they had nothing to suggest but private charity. This state of affairs lasted much longer in Belgium than in France. Throughout Europe in the nineteenth century the *bourgeoisie* or the middle classes rose to power, but in countries like England and France members of the old aristocratic classes still took a prominent part in public affairs and in government. We have seen how some of the early social catholics in France were conservatives of this type, like Villeneuve-Bargemont and Armand de Melun. There were no legitimists in Belgium. There were no natural leaders who were excluded, or self-excluded, from ruling by reason of their royalism and who therefore might find an outlet for their sense of social responsibility in a concern for the welfare of the workers.

In Belgium the *bourgeoisie* had a virtually complete monopoly of power and influence, and so they had everything their own way. They held tenaciously to the dogmas of *laissez faire*, and refused to initiate measures of social legislation, such as the regulation of child labour, until long after they had been accepted in other countries. Since a large proportion of those who wielded political power in Belgium were catholics, catholicism cannot be acquitted of accountability for the blindness and indifference of the ruling classes to the misery by which they were surrounded. Their eyes did not begin to be fully opened till the serious outbreak of proletarian insurrection in 1886, as we shall see in chapter 7.

Social catholicism, then, emerged later and more slowly in Belgium than in France, where from 1830 onwards there were many and varied, if seldom very fruitful, manifestations of it. This, however, lends a special interest to the exceptions that prove the rule, for there were some early social catholics in Belgium. There were three in particular, who deserve to be singled out for remark. They were all laymen and intellectuals, but in other respects they differed from one another.

First, there was Édouard Ducpétiaux (1804-68). He came of a well-known and prosperous family of lace-makers, an industry that belonged more to the past than to the future, and whose interests were different from those of the new capitalist class. Ducpétiaux was all his life free from financial cares, and so at liberty to concern himself with the well-being of society. He had studied law at Liège and Ghent, and had become a convinced believer in liberal institutions and in democracy. He had also acquired a philanthropic idealism and aesthetic sensibilities. He was an adherent of Lamennais. All these traits were calculated to awaken in him a social conscience.

It was as a liberal that he had taken part in the revolution of 1830 when Belgium became independent. He was then appointed Inspector-General of Prisons and Charitable Institutions, a position which he occupied until 1861. Naturally it was a position that offered ample scope for the study of social problems.

Ducpétiaux had been brought up as a catholic, but during the first part of his career he was associated with the liberals rather than with the catholics. He is said to have returned to the practice of religion, partly through the influence of his second wife, and partly in reaction from the growing anti-clericalism of the liberal party. So when unionism—the collaboration of catholics and liberals—at length broke down, Ducpétiaux transferred his allegiance to the conservative or catholic party. But before this, indeed one may say always, his social outlook had had a catholic inspiration.

When he was attacked for joining the conservative party, he replied:

> I am at this moment what I have been from the beginning of my long career: a sincere friend of liberty, as resolved to defend it in the ranks of the so-called clerical party as in those of the liberal party to which I am always proud to have belonged in the time when it was still animated by a spirit of genuine tolerance, when it scrupulously respected religious convictions, and had an equal regard for the spirit and the letter of the Constitution. If, since then, the liberals have gone another way and have adopted another standard, whose fault is that? Am I to be blamed for not having followed them in their anti-catholic crusade?[1]

Liberal anti-clericalism was showing itself especially in a ruthless attempt to secularize education.

Ducpétiaux wrote a number of books on legal and social subjects. Those on the latter show that he was quite definitely a Christian socialist before 1850. He attacked the existing industrial system because it treated men as slaves of machinery. Mechanization, he said, was not bad in itself, but machines were being used solely in the interests of the manufacturers, and not in the interests of workers or of consumers. The appalling contrasts in society between the rich and the poor were contrary to the moral law which directed that men should be brothers and a single family. Unless reform was at once taken in hand there would be a general cataclysm. Thus he wrote in 1843:

> It is impossible to disregard the portents of a new revolution, which will no longer be political, but a social revolution of the poor against the rich, of the proletariat against property. . . . Everywhere there is already a scarcely disguised war of labour against capital, there is anarchy in production, and there is a cold war of taxation: this is all leading up to an open conflict between the workers and the masters, between the producers, and between the nations.[2]

---

[1] Ibid., p. 12.   [2] Ibid., p. 13.

In the face of this state of social disorder and the menace of catastrophe, Ducpétiaux advocated a "homocentric" economy. Production should be for man, not man for production.

The end of man, whatever place he occupies in the human scale, is the free and integral development of his physical, intellectual, and moral faculties. Society, which should be constituted in the interests of all, ought to give man the means of attaining this end.[1]

What was needed was a reordering of society on a basis of co-operation instead of competition. Ducpétiaux derived some of his ideas from Saint-Simon and Fourier. Industry and agriculture should be organized in corporations. He also argued for compulsory education, and such a reform of parliamentary government as would secure representation for the workers and would bring it about that those who voted on measures would in the first instance be those who were most competent to do so, which was not then and is not now a normal feature of parliamentary democracy. We have here the rudiments of the idea of the corporative state which social catholics in Belgium and elsewhere were to work out more fully later on.

Although Ducpétiaux had been influenced by the utopian socialists, he was himself a realist who recognized that it was necessary to start reforms where it was possible to do so. So he urged the need for measures that would regulate child labour, and for the institution of government inspectors who would have power to visit factories at any hour of the day or night. He told employers that it would be to their advantage to have workers who were happy, healthy, and intelligent. He addressed his writings to the *bourgeoisie*, for he realized that they alone were capable of understanding them, owing to the illiteracy of the working class.

A second social catholic in this period was François Huet (1814–69). He was of peasant stock, but his father had taken his

[1] Ibid., p. 14.

young family to try his fortune in Paris. There François was able to receive an advanced education, and from 1835 to 1850 he was professor of philosophy at Ghent University. His religious evolution was in an inverse direction to that of Ducpétiaux. For most of his life he was a practising and devout liberal catholic, but like many other learned and honest men in the nineteenth century he found more and more difficulty in reconciling his scientific knowledge and his philosophical approach to truth with catholic orthodoxy as it was officially presented to him. In 1864 Pius IX's encyclical *Quanta cura* and the *Syllabus errorum* gave the *coup de grâce* to his faith as a catholic, and at the end of his life he was entirely detached from the Church.

The object of his earlier work had been to bring Christianity and socialism together. While he had much in common with the socialists, he had a firm hold on the dogma of original sin which prevented him from indulging in utopian expectations. The concept of "natural law" was basic to his teaching, and from it he inferred that men have a natural right to liberty, equality, and fraternity. But he interpreted them as duties rather than as rights. For example, equality

> requires of men that they never treat their fellows as though they were different in nature or of a different kind, and that they maintain among themselves a material and moral communion.[1]

The object of government is to strengthen society and to preserve it from corruption, by defending what is right.

Huet believed strongly in toleration and in the separation of Church and State. He bitterly attacked the rising ultramontanism which, he said,

> hates only liberty and its martyrs; it eulogizes only despotism and its executioners. It has made the venerable centre of catholic unity the odious citadel of absolutism in Europe, and the successor of the apostles the ally of the kings against the emancipation of Christian

[1] Ibid., pp. 25f.

86

people. . . . The Christian pulpit no longer consoles the poor, and denounces the rich. The degradation of intelligence is accounted the perfection of the law. Spiritual worship is perishing beneath a mass of petty, puerile, and superstitious practices which St Paul would not have known how to condemn strongly enough.[1]

In economic theory, Huet advocated a form of distributivism, which he worked out in detail and which indeed had much to be said for it. But he was a man of ideas rather than of action. He gathered a number of young disciples and a Society-Huet was formed, though it was short-lived.

The third notable Belgian social catholic before 1850 was Adolphe Bartels (1802–62). He was brought up as a protestant, but was converted to catholicism at the age of twenty-two as a result of a visit to Germany. He was primarily a journalist. He was actively engaged in the struggle for Belgian independence. He collaborated in the foundation of the *Avenir*, which was widely read in Belgium. Bartels vigorously attacked the papal encyclical *Mirari vos* which condemned the liberties to which he was passionately attached. But it was not till about 1840 that he realized the importance of the social problem.

In 1842 he published an *Essay on the Organization of Labour* which emphasized the necessity of social, as well as of political, reform. He had a scheme for the introduction of socialism by stages. He drew his ideas indiscriminately from the different schools of utopian socialism. He propagated his ideas through a journal called *Le Débat social* which served as a forum for incipient Christian democrats and for democrats who were not Christians. Among its contributors were Georges Sand, Lamennais, and Louis Blanc. One of its features was entitled "Mouvement des classes ouvrières" which cited all the evidence it could lay hands on that illustrated the determination and attempts of the workers to improve their lot. *Le Débat social* maintained that the only hope for the workers lay in acquiring political power. They could hope

[1] Ibid., pp. 26f.

for nothing from the present ruling classes. History proves, it said, that a class in possession does not voluntarily relinquish power and that, even when some concessions are extorted from it by fear, they are revoked as soon as the peril is passed. Nevertheless, *Le Débat social* did not advocate bloody revolution. Like Huet, Bartels also stood for democratic reform in the structure of the Church, for the election of bishops, and the destruction of the pope's temporal power—measures (he said) that would facilitate the reunion of the Church.

These three Belgian social catholics evidently had much in common with the utopian socialists in their desire for social reorganization, but they were distinguished by their concern for man's moral, intellectual, and spiritual well-being as well as for the amelioration of his material lot. They realized that men must have bread in order to live, but they did not suppose that man can live by bread alone. They may well be described as both Christian socialists and catholic humanists. Further, they were more realistic and pragmatic than most socialists of their time. They were precursors. It was too early yet in Belgium for them to get a real following, and after 1850 Christian socialism was anyhow at a discount, since reaction was everywhere in the ascendant.

For about the next thirty-five years such social catholicism as there was in Belgium was paternalistic in character. That is to say, there was among catholics a certain awareness of social problems that found expression both in practice and in theory, but so far from there being an advance from the incipient Christian socialism which we have been considering there was a reversion from it.

Belgian industry was expanding in this period, and there was an improvement, if only a slight improvement, in the condition of the workers. The catholics shared the *laissez-faire* assumptions of the governing classes and would not hear of any State intervention in industry nor of any workers' organizations that would represent and fight for their interests.

Such catholic attempts as were made to meet the needs of the workers were confined to the formation of circles or guilds that aimed at providing moral and religious influence and charitable relief. Some of these were the outcome of the spread of the Society of St Vincent de Paul into Belgium. In 1862 there were 422 conferences of this society in Belgium with an aggregate membership of nearly 12,000, and the members paid weekly visits to nearly 16,000 poor families.[1] Visiting the families of the poor was, it will be remembered, one of the society's characteristic activities.

Although the Society of St Vincent de Paul was not itself a directly social catholic organization, it did much to create a social conscience and to elicit what may be termed "social vocations" by bringing the sons of the *bourgeoisie* into immediate personal contact with the workers and causing them to see for themselves the miserable conditions in which the poor had to exist.

The undertaking that had most success in this field was the Archconfraternity of St Francis Xavier which was founded in 1854 by a Jesuit named Louis Van Caloen, who realized that laymen must be enlisted in an apostolate to the workers. The object of the confraternity was to form faithful and instructed Christians who would give themselves to the conversion of sinners through getting to know them in their homes or in the public houses. The élite of the members were known as Père Van Caloen's "gun dogs". During the twenty-five years following 1854, they are said to have been responsible for 13,478 conversions, for regularizing nearly 5,000 marriages, for distributing 150,000 good books, and for destroying over 12,000 bad books. Pilgrimages and other pious activities were organized and libraries and night-schools were formed, wherever branches of the

[1] Ibid., p. 50.

confraternity were established. At Malines, for instance, 15,000 books were borrowed from the library in 1866. The number of members steadily increased until the 1880s—from the fifteen foundation members in 1854 to 8,300 members in 1879 who were organized in 342 branches.[1]

While these figures are by no means contemptible, it should be noted that this society does not seem to have succeeded in the large industrial centres, but rather in the small towns, and its members were drawn chiefly from the petty-*bourgeoisie*—artisans, shopkeepers, bailiffs, and the like. In the official report for 1867–8 we read:

> It seems that the efforts made in an industrial centre to found an association whose members would have a certain degree of faith failed to come to anything, because of the almost complete absence of moral and religious instruction.[2]

Societies similar to the Archconfraternity of St Francis Xavier were established, such as a Society of St Joseph in 1855, and in 1871 they were affiliated to one another in a "Federation of Catholic Workers' Societies".

The original motive of these societies was a moral one, namely to raise the moral standards of the workers and of their families: but in order to acquire any influence they found that they needed to provide social, educational, and recreational services, savings clubs, and charitable relief. Obviously, their appeal would be to the most docile of the poor. Even where they did get some roots in the world of industry proper, they failed to hold their ground after the foundation of the first International by Marx and Engels in 1864. This event more than anything else stirred the spirit of independence among the Belgian workers and gave them courage to believe that they must depend on their own efforts for their emancipation. "Patronage" and paternalistic organizations had no attraction for men who were seized by

[1] Ibid., pp. 52ff.   [2] Ibid., p. 55.

a determination to achieve their rights. From this time then the workers were increasingly drawn into the socialist movement.

The catholic societies, on the other hand, were sometimes supported even by non-Christian industrialists, precisely because they could be expected to serve as a brake on socialist agitation and violence, since the catholics were opposed to all militant measures on the part of the workers. Thus in 1867 we find an industrialist saying:

> I believe that the best way of preventing the recurrence of strikes, and above all of depriving them of their demagogic character, would be to establish . . . an Association of St Francis Xavier. . . . If Père Van Caloen would come and propagate it among us, he would be welcomed with enthusiasm, and the heads of industry would themselves lend him a hand.[1]

The catholics, on their part, boasted that no member of their circles had taken part in a strike or in socialist demonstrations. In short, the industrialists were prepared to support any associations that accepted the existing order and confined themselves to purely palliative, non-political activities. It has been said that whereas the catholic socialists before 1848 had ideas but no followers, afterwards the paternalist social catholics had a certain number of followers but hardly any ideas.[2]

Still, there was an ideology of sorts underlying catholic paternalism in Belgium, or at least there was an attitude. It acknowledged that there were social evils that ought to be remedied. But it assumed that they could be remedied only by moralizing and charitable activities. There was a fixed opposition to State action. It was taken for granted that God had ordained the division between rich and poor. The rich ought to help the poor; the poor ought to respect and serve the rich. It was an ideology of duty, not of rights.

[1] Ibid., p. 62.   [2] Ibid., pp. 66f.

As a catholic orator put it in 1870:

> Happy are the artisans who do their duty, who love God and their work, who know how to save and to co-operate with one another. Happy are the rich who understand their earthly mission and devote themselves to the noble task of supporting those whom God has placed beneath them in the ordering of this world.[1]

So the ideal employer is to regard his employees as a father regards his family. He should interest himself in their concerns, pay their wages regularly, look to the safety, hygiene, and morality of his factory, punish those who flaunt his authority, and give them sound instruction. The ideal worker is to be honest and orderly, docile, and religious, a good family man, keen on his work: he will regard his employer's interests as his own. If both employers and employees did their duty according to these ideals, harmony and prosperity would be the result.

It may be that this kind of teaching had some salutary effect on employers, but it was really no more than a survival of traditional ideas. It was a doctrine that failed to engage with the realities of the industrial world.

This was in effect confessed to be the case by the founder of the Society of St Joseph who said in 1871:

> We have achieved nothing so far; we have won a few hundred men, but what do these numbers represent in regard to the working population? As good as nothing . . . In fact, the influence of the clergy and of lay catholics on the industrial workers is to all intents and purposes *nil*. Why? Is it not because so far the method used in order to win the confidence of the masses has too exclusively been to preach to them always about their duties without ever telling them about their rights?[2]

This appears to be a just verdict on the paternalistic form of social catholicism.

Paternalism held the field in Belgium as in France at this time,

[1] Ibid., p. 74.   [2] Ibid., p. 78.

but even so there were already the beginnings of a new approach that would later develop into the powerful Christian democrat movement towards the close of the century. At first, only a tiny minority of catholics started to penetrate deeper into the realities of the social situation. They realized that the working class did not want paternal protection and was becoming capable of organizing itself. They refused to accept the assumptions of *laissez faire* and began to demand reforms in the structure of industrial society. They looked to the State to intervene. They did not look upon the division between rich and poor as divinely ordained, nor did they pretend that the interests of employers and employed were the same. They saw that workers as well as capitalists should have their own organizations to represent their different interests. Finally, they gave up talking about charity and spoke of rights and justice.

Where did this new minority of social catholics make its appearance? I pointed out that Belgian independence had been achieved in 1830 by the united efforts of the liberals and the catholics, and they continued to collaborate in the early years of the new State. But as time went on this alliance was subjected to too much strain for it to last. In particular, the liberal party was becoming increasingly anti-clerical, like the liberal parties in other continental countries.

At the elections in 1857, to the cry of "Down with the priests", the liberal party won seventy seats, while the catholics had only thirty-eight. This shook up the catholics. They were in for a bitter struggle, especially in the field of education. What they really needed to do was to rethink their political philosophy and to produce a new programme. But the conservatives as a whole were stuck in the mud. It was a perception that this was so that induced some younger catholics to try their hand at furnishing the catholic party with a new reformist and progressive policy. To this end they launched a new journal, *L'Universel*. It was actually founded by Jules Gondon who had been on the editorial

staff of the *Univers* in Paris. But he had fallen out with Louis
Veuillot, and in 1859 he arrived in Brussels resolved to get a
group of young writers together who were devoted to the cause
of liberty and social justice.

The leader of this group was Prosper de Haulleville (b. 1830).
He was of aristocratic descent and had had a voltairian upbringing. He owed his catholic conversion to Lacordaire whom he
heard preach at Liège. He had a distinguished academic career
and at the age of twenty-seven was appointed professor of
natural law at the University of Ghent. But after the victory of
the liberal party he was deprived of his chair, and so was set free
to engage in political agitation and journalism.

The group of young catholics who gathered round him
formed a new left-wing element in the catholic or conservative
party. They came to be known as "la Jeune-Droite". They were
encouraged by Ducpétiaux and a few of the earlier social
catholics. In *L'Universel* they put forward a programme that was
politically liberal, similar to that of the *Avenir* in 1830–1. But
they went further than the *Avenir* and the liberal catholics. In the
interest of the workers, they pressed for the gradual introduction
of universal suffrage, for the abolition of the laws which prohibited the organization of the workers in trade unions, and for a
number of similar measures. In 1861 they said of themselves:

> In our country we are regarded, not without reason, as the pro-
> pagators of frankly progressive ideas, of ideas that are prudently
> conservative, perfectly practicable and qualified to affect for good
> the present policy of our country and the opinions of the electors . . .
> The *Universel* is the only considerable journal edited by catholics,
> that is really feared by the liberal sects. [1]

It was this group, together with Ducpétiaux who was still
alive, which started a ferment in the Catholic Congresses that
were held at Malines in 1863 and 1864, when they tried to get the
principle of a living wage recognized. But they were so fiercely

[1] Ibid., pp. 83f.

attacked by the conservative elements in the catholic party that they found it difficult to get a hearing.

However, although they were a minority and failed to get their programme adopted by the party, they succeeded in disturbing its complacency about the social problem. They began to educate it in the need for a combative social policy that would appeal to, and meet the needs of, the working classes through State intervention and legislation. Thus we have in Belgium around 1870 the seed-bed of a catholic democratic movement.

It was not to begin to come to fruition till after 1886 which, as we shall see, was a turning-point in Belgian social history. By that time the ideas of the Belgian social catholics had been enriched through contact with their opposite numbers in Germany and France.

PART TWO

5

Germany

The story of social catholicism in Germany[1] has a comparatively late beginning since industrialization did not take place so soon as in England, France, or Belgium. The story can also be told more briefly, because it was happier, more straightforward and less beset by cross-currents.

After the upheavals of the French Revolution and the Napoleonic wars the Catholic Church in Germany was at a low ebb. The Holy Roman Empire had broken up; the Prince-bishops had been deprived of their temporal power; and in the reorganization of the German states catholics in many places found themselves subject to protestant rulers. Representative governments and constitutional liberties had not been established. The political authorities inherited the attitude of the Emperor Joseph II to the relations of Church and State: that is to say, they had a high view of the rôle of princes in ecclesiastical affairs.

Moreover, in the Church itself there was a definitely josephist or febronian school of thought which favoured the formation of a German National Catholic Church that would be only loosely attached to the papacy. This movement was, however, unsuccessful, and indeed had an opposite effect from what it intended, for

[1] See Edgar Alexander on "Church and Society in Germany" in *Church and Society: Catholic Social and Political Thought and Movements, 1789–1950*, ed. by J. N. Moody (New York, 1953), pp. 325–583; Georges Goyau, *L'Allemagne religieuse: Le Catholicisme*, 4 vols. (Paris, 1909–10).

it provoked the growth of ultramontanism. One of the principal factors that inspired nineteenth-century ultramontanism was the hope that the papacy would be able to prevent the Church from being controlled or exploited by civil rulers. It was not foreseen that the power of the papacy itself might turn into an alternative kind of despotism which would be hardly less inimical to the liberty of national churches. Churchmen are always liable to overlook the fact that ecclesiastics are just as likely to abuse power as statesmen.

In all the German states around 1830 there was more or less constant friction between the Church and civil governments. The activities of the Church were confined or impeded by the attempts of the princes to limit and control ecclesiastical authority, while on the other hand the popes were all the time trying to secure what they regarded as the basic rights of the Church. The main question at issue was that of mixed marriages, that is between catholics and protestants. This question was especially acute in Prussia, and in 1837 led to a crisis in which Mgr Droste-Vischering (1773-1845), Archbishop of Cologne, was imprisoned for refusing to comply with the will of the Government. This event, which made a profound impression and strengthened the Church's position—as the witness of martyrs usually does—has even been described as the most important event since the Reformation, since it demonstrated that the Church was independent of the State and not its tool. Anyhow, this event may be said to signalize the beginning of the catholic revival in Germany which was such a striking feature of the second half of the nineteenth century. None the less, the Church continued to be hampered and restricted in most of the states until 1848, the year of revolutions, when at last absolute governments were overthrown or at least compelled to grant constitutions and civil liberties.

The oppression of the Church by the civil rulers had fostered among the catholics both liberalism, in the sense of a zest for liberty, and ultramontanism or emphasis on the rôle of the papacy in defending the liberty of the Church. The catholics took advantage of the freedom which they were now able to claim in order to set in motion a general revival of church life. The Church was fortunate in that a leader arose to match the hour, Wilhelm Emmanuel von Ketteler (1811–77),[1] who is of special importance in our present context because, among other things, he was outstanding as a social catholic. There had indeed already been a German catholic whose teaching about social justice had been far in advance of his times—Franz von Baader (1765–1841).[2] He was a friend of Lamennais. He was neglected by his compatriots in the nineteenth century and it is only recently that his prophetic qualities have come to be recognized.

Ketteler came of an old aristocratic family with feudal traditions, from which he derived a keen sense of the responsibility of the strong for the weak. He was not educated for the ministry of the Church, nor as a young man was he notably devout. He entered the Prussian civil service, but soon reacted violently against its despotic methods. The turning-point in his career was the Prussian government's arrest in 1837 of the Archbishop of Cologne on account of his refusal to submit to its demands. Ketteler was so shocked by this oppressive action that he resigned from the civil service, and subsequently decided to devote himself to the service of the Church as a priest. After studying theology at Munich, he entered the seminary at Münster at the age of thirty-two, and in due course became a parish priest.

Thereafter he identified himself with the interests of the common people. He accused the aristocracy of being a caricature of itself and of being attached to its titles while it had deserted its social functions and duties. In 1848 he emerged as a leading catholic spokesman, both in the Parliament at Frankfurt of which he was elected a member (taking his seat on the extreme

[1] See Georges Goyau, *Ketteler* (Paris, 1908).
[2] See Alexander, op. cit., pp. 393–406, 415.

left as Lacordaire had done in the National Assembly at Paris) and at the Catholic Congress which was held at Mainz at this time, and also in his sermons and addresses on special occasions.

At the Catholic Congress he echoed the language of Lamennais and the *Avenir*:

> Religion has nothing to fear from liberty. On the contrary, thanks to liberty, religion will appear in its true lustre. Doubtless, liberty takes away from religion the protection of men and the support of the State. But that is not at all the protection it was promised. It is assured of divine protection, which will be all the stronger when it is without human protection. Religion can do nothing but rejoice in liberty, for under its reign it will deploy all its strength and the splendour of truth, and error will give way so soon as it is deprived of the support of the secular power. But as religion needs liberty, so does liberty need religion. Anyone who has carefully studied the present situation cannot fail to see that, if the people do not return to religion, they will not be capable of maintaining liberty. Only the Church and Christianity make man capable of complete liberty.[1]

Ketteler was indeed a great *liberal* catholic, and he was destined to be a leader of the minority at the Vatican Council in 1870. He was also a great church reformer, and the diocese of Mainz, of which he was made bishop in 1850, became a model diocese. But here we are concerned only with his *social* catholicism.

Already in 1848 preaching in Mainz cathedral, two years before he became bishop, he showed that he stood for a Christian social doctrine that was different from both *laissez-faire* liberalism and state socialism.

> The famous saying, "Property is robbery", is not just a lie: it contains, alongside a great lie, a fruitful truth. [And he went on to describe as a] "perpetual crime against nature" the modern conception that makes a proprietor an absolute sovereign of his

[1] See Goyau, *Ketteler*, pp. 29f.

possessions, dispensed from every social function, cut off from all responsibility.[1]

And again in another sermon at this time he said:

No one can say anything about our era or comprehend its shape without referring again and again to the prevailing social conditions and, above all, to the division between the propertied and the property-less classes, to the plight of our destitute brethren, to the means of giving them help. You may accord as much weight as you please to the political questions, to the shaping of state and government—and yet, the real difficulties we face do not lie there. . . . Paradoxically, the closer we carry our political problems toward bearable solutions the clearer it becomes, though many will not see it even now, that this was only the lesser part of the task before us and that now the social question looms larger than ever, demanding solutions more harshly than ever.[2]

I shall have more to say about the development of Ketteler's teaching and action presently. It is important to bear in mind that the coming of the Industrial Revolution in Germany was retarded. As Sir John Clapham said:

The states which were to become Imperial Germany showed an exceedingly low level of industrialisation in 1815, and a level very little higher in 1850. . . . Even in those parts of Germany best fitted for industrial development, such as Saxony and the new Rhenish provinces of Prussia, there was no rapid movement. For fifteen years at least after Waterloo the dislocations due to war and peace acted as a drag on progress. There was no tradition of individual industrial enterprise or of large scale operations. Capital was scarce . . . Industrial freedom was not yet guaranteed . . . Political questions occupied men's minds. The political divisions and rivalries of the German states limited the possible scale of industrial operations.[3]

[1] See Goyau, *L'Allemagne religieuse*, ii, 400.
[2] See Alexander, op. cit., p. 408.
[3] Clapham, *Economic Development of France and Germany, 1815-1914*, pp. 82, 88.

In 1837 Berlin had only thirty steam engines averaging 13 h.p. each, and the coal output of Germany in 1846 was only about half that of Belgium. Two cities in France had a combined population of any twelve German cities. The German workers remained peasants and handicraftsmen till a much later date than in other western countries. All these circumstances, together with the fact that the problems created by industrialism came to a head only at a time when conditions were favourable to a revival of catholic missionary enterprise and activity, help to explain the impressive quality and the large influence of the social catholic movement in this country. The Church used the opportunities that opened before it after 1848 not only to secure its own rights but to convey to the German people the idea of a Christian social order as a live option.

Furthermore, from 1848 onwards the catholic congresses, which were under lay leadership, gave the catholic laity the sense that they had an active, and not merely a passive or docile, part to play in the Church's mission to the nation. One of the consequences of this early enfranchisement of the laity in responsibility for the mission of the Church was seen in the *Kulturkampf* of 1870–87. The Church was able to resist Bismarck's campaign against it stoutly, and in the end successfully, because it had acquired real roots in the life of the nation, not least, as we shall see, among the workers.

Before returning to Ketteler, I want to say a little about another man who made a remarkable contribution to social catholicism in Germany, namely Adolph Kolping (1813–65). Kolping, unlike Ketteler, was born of poor parents and became a shoemaker. In those days, German craftsmen and tradesmen had to undergo the traditional training as apprentices and journeymen, before they could qualify as master-workmen. As journeymen they travelled from one town to another, finding work in each place and learning different skills that were employed in different localities. In France this was spoken of as doing the

Tour de France. Before the French Revolution, journeymen throughout Europe had had their own associations or guilds which provided accommodation and other amenities as they travelled from place to place. These associations had more or less been driven underground, if not destroyed during the revolutionary era. In consequence the young journeymen were liable to be uprooted, feckless, and corrupted.

Kolping, who had himself experienced their lot as a travelling shoemaker, determined to do something to provide them with a counterpart to family life and with the support of the Church. It was with this aim he sought to become a priest. But he had much difficulty in acquiring the necessary qualifications for ordination, and it was not until 1845, when he was thirty-two years of age, that he could embark on his life's work. He set himself to establish a network of Young Catholic Workmen's Societies which would serve the moral, religious, technical, and cultural interests of young journeymen. His headquarters were at Cologne where he was an assistant priest at the cathedral, but with apostolic zeal he travelled all over Germany forming, wherever possible, branches of his society with hostels. Each branch had a resident priest-president.

When Kolping died in 1865, there were 400 branches and the movement continued to grow. The methods adopted were similar to those which we now associate with the Y.M.C.A. and the Jeunesse Ouvrière Chrétienne (Jocists). While there were definite rules about worship and religious instruction, Kolping's movement also sought to enable its members to improve their professional skill and their cultural education and to give them a high sense of civic responsibility. By its means there was built up a large and united body of respected master-workmen, who remained sincerely attached to the Church and to the clergy. It was a movement which social catholics in other countries, when they learned about it, desired to emulate. All his life Kolping continued to be a genuine man of the people, who was able to speak their language and to respect their sensibilities. A similar work for agricultural workers was set on foot by a former army officer named Alst (1825–95). It must not be forgotten that the social catholic leadership of Ketteler was, as it were, underpinned by these pervasive forms of catholic action.

Ketteler himself had begun by preaching a regeneration of society through the consecration of individual lives to the service of the community, but he came to realize more and more the need to establish social structures that would be favourable to a Christian order. In 1864 he developed his ideas in a book on *The Labour Question and Christianity*, relating them to the two principal programmes for social reform that were being advocated in Germany at the time—liberalism and socialism.

He first exposed the intolerable position of the workers under *laissez-faire* capitalism which, he said, reduced them to wage slavery. Then he examined the proposed remedies of the liberal and socialist reformers. Both proposed the creation of co-operative production associations as the means of rescuing working men from dependence on the wage system. The liberals, represented by Schultse-Delitzch (1808–83), defended liberty of industry and trade, repudiated State intervention, and trusted to self-help on the part of the workers themselves. Co-operative associations were to be formed voluntarily with capital contributed from the savings of the members. This proposal, Ketteler said, was wholly inadequate. Only the most prosperous artisans were in a position to act upon it. The wage-earners in the larger industries had no prospect of accumulating sufficient capital to launch co-operative societies.

Ketteler then turned to the socialists and their magnetic leader, Ferdinand Lassalle (1825–64). Lassalle was the creator of the German socialist party, which subsequently became marxist. During his short-lived period of leadership he was immensely popular. Wherever he went, the working masses erected triumphal arches and working girls threw flowers at his feet. His plan was for the State to provide the capital for co-operative societies of production. Ketteler allowed that the socialists undoubtedly had the merit of having depicted, in terms that were as forcible as they were true, the situation of the working classes, and he accepted on the whole their criticism of the existing system.

He could not, however, accept their positive or constructive proposals. Ketteler, ever after his experience in the Prussian civil service, was mistrustful of government and of bureaucratic centralization, and therefore of State socialism. Moreover, at this time he held that the government had no moral right to take the wealth of some citizens and to lend it to others. He feared that the State would thus domineer over the rich by its fiscal exactions and over the poor by its gratuitous favours. His own proposal was that co-operative societies should be financed by the voluntary contributions of Christians. In the old days the Church had raised large sums for the building of cathedrals: why not now for the reform of the industrial system?

His book had a large success and was favourably reviewed in the catholic press. It went through three editions in a year, and letters of gratitude poured in upon the author from people of all classes and creeds. Lassalle himself went out of his way to applaud it. Addressing a socialist gathering at Ronsdorf on 23 May 1864, he said:

> Recently a prince of the church, the Bishop of Mainz, pressed by his conscience, has intervened in the workers' question. . . . On point after point, he adopts my proposals and my economic theses and rejects those of the progressives [i.e. of the liberals] with penetration and frankness. You know, my friends, that I do not belong to the category of pious folk. But it is only just that I should assign the greatest value to this testimony . . . A bishop finds himself in conscience bound to express himself with the same severity that I as a tribune of the people am free to use . . . ?[1]

In France *Le Temps* reviewed Ketteler's book under the title "A

[1] See Goyau, *L'Allemagne religieuse*, iii, 141.

Socialist Bishop", an expression which at that time seemed like a contradiction in terms.

Ketteler had in fact a great regard for Lassalle. In January 1864 a curious letter, bearing a Frankfurt postmark, reached Lassalle at Berlin. The writer did not give his name but gave a poste restante address for a reply. He said that he had at his disposal 50,000 florins and he was thinking of using this capital to found five small co-operative associations, which seemed to him preferable to intervention by the State, and he asked Lassalle for his advice about the project. Lassalle replied sympathetically, and then it turned out that Ketteler was the writer of the letter.

Ketteler's own policy became more radical and more precise. In 1869 he plainly told the workers that their demands for higher wages, for shorter hours, for holidays, for the prohibition of child labour and of the industrial employment of women, were sanctioned by justice and by Christianity, and could be satis-factorily met only if they were harnessed to the precepts of religion and morality. Otherwise workers would be corruped by the unbridled materialism which was the cause of their present hardships. He also commended the achievements of the English trade unions.

In the same year he prepared a report for the meeting of the German bishops at Fulda in which he said that the social question was more acute and more serious than any other. He gave a powerful exposition of what the problem was and what the Church ought to do. This report was splendidly definite and free from the vague platitudinizing that has marked too many Christian statements on this subject. Ketteler not only made specific proposals but urged that priests as well as laymen should be set apart and trained to translate them into practice.

The Church must stimulate the interest of the clergy in the fate of the working classes. They have mostly little interest in these matters because they are ignorant of the existence and the impact of the dangers which lurk in these threatening social conditions, because they have failed to size up the character and breadth of the social question, finally, because they have no conception of possible remedies. The labour problem must therefore no longer be neglected in the education of the clergy. . . . It would be desirable if selected clerics were directed toward the study of economics and given travelling stipends so that they might become acquainted through their own observation with the needs of labour on the one hand, and with existing welfare services on the other.[1]

Although the other bishops were not at once persuaded to accept this recommendation, Ketteler himself acted upon his precepts in his own diocesan seminary and through periodical literature, and in consequence a growing body of socially trained priests was built up.

By this time Ketteler, although he remained convinced that Christianity rather than the State must take the lead in promoting the reorganization of industry, had come to see the necessity of labour legislation by government. His overriding passion for social justice and reform overcame his deep distrust of the power of the State. In 1873 he drew up a programme for the German catholics at the time of the establishment of the German Empire. It became the basis of the social policies of the centre party, which became the chief medium of catholic social and political pressure. He demanded the restoration to the workers of the right to form their own corporative organizations. It was the duty of the State to secure to the workers protection from the hazards of the capitalist system, and he specified indispensable measures, such as the institution of a scheme of factory inspection, that would ensure that protective legislation was actually carried out.

Ketteler, who died in 1877, is the greatest figure in nineteenth-century social catholicism, and Leo XIII acknowledged his indebtedness to him when preparing his famous encyclical *Rerum novarum*.[2] In twentieth-century England it may seem that

[1] See Alexander, op. cit., p. 416. [2] See p. 127f. below.

he bears a strong resemblance to William Temple, but with the difference that he started a social movement that grew into a powerful political force in the life of his country, and it is still influential to-day, for the present Christian democrat party in Germany is descended from it.

Ketteler was succeeded as leader by Christopher Moufang (1817–90), a priest who was a protégé of Ketteler, and who went beyond him in pressing for labour legislation. The fact that the centre party had a progressive social policy, which was regarded as dangerous by both the conservative and the liberal parties, was a reason, though only a subsidiary one, for the hostility to the catholics which they displayed during the *Kulturkampf*. During the *Kulturkampf*, which was in itself evidence of the influence that the catholic Church in Germany had acquired in the period from 1848 to 1870, the main concern of the catholics was inevitably the defence of their political and ecclesiastical rights.

In 1886 Moufang was succeeded in the leadership by another priest, Franz Hitze (1851–1921), who at the outset of his political career in 1880 had described his aims as follows:

Now began a new philosophy and a new program for my life with the aim of devoting all my strength to the lifting up of these masses (of the workers) by means of a comprehensive *social reform*, systematic institutions for their education and self-training, to make them economically, morally and mentally capable of *co-operating in state and society* as mature and responsible persons.[1]

Hitze organized the catholic labour movement and won for it an essential place in the whole Christian labour movement of Germany which was interconfessional. In spite of opposition from integrist and clerically minded catholics, he gathered the overwhelming majority of catholic workers into the ranks of the Christian trade unions where they could work successfully for constructive social policies. In the Reichstag the centre party

[1] See Alexander, op. cit., p. 427.

promoted legislation for social reform in a thoroughly realistic way. Social catholic ideas also found expression in periodicals and in the catholic press. They were discussed regularly at the catholic congresses and they inspired a large complex of organizations. Indeed, social catholics in other countries looked to Germany with admiration and envy.

6

France: 1870-1920[1]

The only social catholicism that had survived in France under the Second Empire was, as we saw in chapter 3, that of the right: it was conservative and grounded in the thesis of the Counter-Revolution. This was still the case in the early years of the Third Republic. The downfall of the Empire, the defeat of France by Germany, and above all the experience of the Commune in Paris in 1872, naturally intensified the fears that the conservative classes already entertained of what they vaguely called "socialism". In 1872 the National Assembly appointed a commission to inquire into the condition of the workers. All the members of this commission were practising catholics. It reported that the condition of the workers was all that it could be expected to be and nothing could be done about it.[2]

The catholics had of course special motives to reaction at this time. The communards had confiscated the property of the religious orders, and had taken other steps against religion. Among the hostages they had massacred had been Archbishop Darboy and a number of priests. Socialism, it seemed, was the declared enemy of religion as well as of property.

---

[1] For this period see Henri Rollet, *L'Action sociale des catholiques en France, 1871–1901* (1947); Georges Hoog, *Histoire du catholicisme social en France, 1871–1931* (1946); J. Brugerette, *Le Prêtre Français et la Société Contemporaine*, vols. ii and iii (1935–8); P. T. Moon, *The Labor Problem and the Social Catholic Movement in France;* A. Dansette, *Religious History of Modern France.*

[2] See Brugerette, op. cit., ii, 374.

However, not all French catholics reacted in a purely negative way. It was just at this time that two young officers, both of them aristocrats, were moved to dedicate themselves to the social catholic cause with far-reaching results—Count Albert de Mun (1841–1914) and Count René de la Tour du Pin (1834–1925). They were both taken prisoner in the Franco-Prussian war and were interned at Aix-la-Chapelle. There, in November 1870, they discussed the disaster that had befallen their country and asked what had caused it. They found what they thought to be the answer in a book that came into their hands while they were in captivity, and that made a deep and lasting impression on them.

It was a book entitled *The Encyclical of 8 December 1864 and the Principles of 1789 or the Church, the State and Liberty* which had been published in 1865. The author's name was Émile Keller (1828–1909).[1] I am going to deal with him and his book at some length, since to do so will bring into clear light the fundamental beliefs of the conservative social catholics, beliefs which it is difficult for English readers to appreciate. Keller was an Alsatian, the son of a judge at Belfort, who died when Émile was an infant. His mother took him to Paris for his education, where he made his way to the École Polytechnique. He was a man of scholarly bent: for instance, in 1858 he published a history of France. He was intensely patriotic and extremely catholic, an ultramontane in the tradition of de Maistre. In 1859 he was elected a deputy and soon made a mark by his eloquent defence of the pope's temporal power.

One day in December 1864 he had occasion to call on the papal nuncio in Paris, and saw that he had a pile of envelopes on his desk about which he was obviously much embarrassed. It appeared that one of these envelopes was addressed to each of the French bishops and ought to be delivered without delay. But the nuncio dare not send them by post. The government would probably intercept them, since these were documents that had

[1] On Keller, see Gustave Gautherot, *Émile Keller* (1922).

come from Rome. Keller immediately offered to take charge of them and undertook that they would be delivered by hand within forty-eight hours to all the bishops. He recalled afterwards that the nuncio had hardly been able to believe his ears but, being only too glad to be relieved of his burden, he had handed the envelopes over. Keller thereupon summoned some young men who were associated with him and devoted to the ultramontane cause. The railway time-tables were consulted and journeys were worked out that would cover all the dioceses. The result was that within three days all the documents had reached their destination and the couriers were back in Paris without anyone knowing how the pope's intention had been carried out.

The documents were of course the encyclical *Quanta cura* and the *Syllabus errorum*, Pius IX's summary exposure of all the modern errors: rationalism, socialism, materialism, gallicanism, liberalism, secularism. It seemed to most people that the pope had condemned *en bloc* all the principles of contemporary civilization and all the liberties. The Syllabus, said a French anti-clerical paper, was "the supreme challenge thrown at the modern world by the expiring papacy".[1] Napoleon III's government denounced the papal acts and took measures against two of the bishops who had had the documents read from the pulpit.

The liberal catholics were gravely disconcerted, since it seemed that all that they had been saying about the virtues of political liberty and liberty of conscience and "the free church in the free state" had been condemned by the pope. In order to ease the situation, Dupanloup hurriedly wrote a commentary on the encyclical in which he explained away its prima facie meaning, and Pius IX, who had been taken aback by the way his pronouncements had been received, appeared to give his countenance to Dupanloup's enterprise.

Émile Keller, however, was more of an ultramontane than the pope himself, and had no wish for any mitigation of the plain

[1] Op. cit., p. 125.

meaning of the papal utterances. His book, published in 1865, was a rejoinder to Dupanloup. To Keller it seemed that Dupanloup was treating the teaching of the encyclical as still-born, or was relegating it to a platonic plane (that of the "thesis" as distinguished from the "hypothesis") where it had nothing to do with the contemporary state of affairs. So with studied irony Keller wrote in retrospect about what he had himself done on this occasion:

> Mgr Dupanloup found a splendid occasion for correcting a blunder that Pius IX had made and for rescuing the Holy See and the Church from the storm which seemed to threaten them. In his commentary which was disseminated throughout the world and translated into all languages, he proved that there was no need to change anything in the life or habits or liberties of modern peoples: the Church should accommodate itself to their institutions and their laws, as it had done to those of protestant, schismatic and infidel peoples among whom it had been compelled to live. . . .
>
> Since I was convinced in my humble sphere that the condemnations pronounced by Pius IX had a significance which ought not to be set aside, that they met the needs and dangers of the present time, and that only a return to a Christian régime could save a society on its last legs, I tried in a small volume to show, from a lay and political standpoint, not what the encyclical was not, but what it really was and the consequences that we ought to deduce from it. [1]

The "small volume" was a major work of nearly 450 pages. It invites comparison with Gladstone's early work, *The State in its Relations with the Church*.[2] That is to say, it is an argument for a thoroughgoing Christian conservatism which tries to take into account the realities of the nineteenth century: but there are these differences. Keller's book was better written and more readable, and whereas Gladstone soon abandoned his "stern and unbending toryism", Keller stuck to his guns for the rest of his

[1] Ibid., pp. 125f. [2] See my book, *The Orb and the Cross* (1945).

life and was putting a new edition (but not an altered edition) of his book through the press when he died in 1909.

The striking thing about his book is that, so far from being an apology for the papal documents or an attempt to make the best of them, they are declared to be in every respect a courageous assertion of the only social and political philosophy that is true and that offers a return to health for peoples who have been led astray by "the Revolution", i.e. by all the ideas of which 1789 was the symbol. The pope is extolled as a prophetic voice who has boldly confronted the popular illusions of the age—the rights of reason, the sovereignty of the people, liberty of conscience, the separation of Church and State—with the truth for which the Christian tradition has always stood, namely, the sovereignty of God, the infallible authority of Christ's Vicar, the dependence of the political order upon the spiritual order, and of morality upon Christian doctrine. It was a case of *Pius contra mundum*.

Keller works out his theme with a survey of the history of Christendom, maintaining that the Roman Church has always been the source and safeguard of social health and of real liberty. Heresy, schism, protestantism, rationalism, and liberalism have been corrosive and demoralizing in their effects, and so far from producing personal and communal liberty have issued in anarchy and despotism. It was only necessary to look beneath the vaunted material prosperity and progress of the nineteenth century to find great centralized bureaucracies which were indifferent to the life of the spirit and to the moral principles upon which social and political health depends.

> Local liberties are disappearing. Communes and provinces are giving place to a clever bureaucracy that dispenses everyone from the need to think and act, and that accumulates at the centre of some great states the care and responsibility for everything. In the sphere of labour, this centralization suppresses the small industries, ensures the triumph of the large capitalists, and creates on the one hand a veritable financial feudalism, and

on the other increases ever more and more the numbers of the proletariat.[1]

It is the Revolution that, by dethroning God and jettisoning the authority of his law and his Church, has given free course to individual egoism and unbridled licence. What the sovereignty of the people means in effect is the sovereignty of those who happen to possess or to gain power and property, and who usurp the place of the divinely ordained guardians of a moral order. The Revolution says to the people:

> L'État, c'est toi! Because no rights are sacred, it is no longer the good pleasure of the prince, it is your good pleasure that will make law, that will create justice, that will dictate truth. The king was only your representative, your delegate whom you could recall when you wished; henceforth you will yourself be an absolute infallible sovereign.[2]

Or again:

> Far from doing away with the proletariat, the Revolution created it. It began and has increased the division of society into two classes—on the one side, those who have nothing and who, never being sure of the morrow, live from day to day by their labour; on the other side, those who possess capital, i.e. the instruments of labour, land, money, machines, and who thereby are at once independent and masters of the workers' fate . . .
>
> In France . . . in a few years, the number of proletarians has increased by about three million and the number of agricultural workers has decreased accordingly. Thus the evil is progressive . . .[3]

It was silly to say that the workers were free. The only people who were free were those who were already rich.

> What does the freedom of the man who has nothing really amount to? Education, which is the first thing he needs, is accessible only to men whose circumstances permit them to get it. . . . The ele-

[1] Keller, L'Encyclique etc, p. 33.   [2] Op. cit., p. 198.
[3] Ibid., p. 251.

117

mentary instruction, which society offers (the child of the proletarian), is only a mockery, since, in order to live, he is condemned
to use up his growing strength, his intelligence, and his character,
in the factories to which hunger drives him. . . .

When he becomes a man, is the worker really free to choose a
trade . . .? All skilled work requires a professional education, a
time for study and apprenticeship . . . which is impossible for the
poor. The case is still worse if it is a question of becoming really
independent, of working on his own account, of buying a shop or
building up a business. Even if by dint of sacrifices you managed to
start a business . . . lo and behold, in the name of liberty, you will
find that a powerful manufacturer will come and establish himself
next door to you, armed with capital and machinery . . . with
whom it is impossible for you to compete. . . . Everywhere the
large shops and factories devour the little ones.[1]

It was passages like these that moved the two young officers at
Aix-la-Chapelle, and above all Keller's chapter on "Social Truth
as the Principle of Social liberty" in which he outlined a social
order that would give a fuller life and genuine liberty to the
workers by enabling them to become independent, and by
safeguarding their family life, their education, and their Sunday
rest. Keller called for men who would devote themselves, as the
Benedictines had of old, to renewing the Christian foundations
of the social order. Addressing himself to the workers, he said:

Workers, who fight against poverty, and who preserve amid your
toils the legitimate sense of your dignity, do not seek to separate
your cause from that of the Vicar of Jesus Christ. It was the Church
alone that began, and it will be the Church alone that will complete, your emancipation. Your destiny is intimately joined to hers.
When she is persecuted, oppressed, reduced to a pittance or to
slavery, you will be with her. On the other hand, her triumph will
be the signal of yours, and her complete liberty will be the assurance
of your independence.[2]

[1] Ibid., pp. 254ff.   [2] Ibid., p. 406.

The conviction, the persuasive confidence, the urgency of Keller's writing, together with the incisiveness of his style, were well calculated to impress young men who had just been shaken into seriousness by the disasters that had befallen their country. Other experiences were to follow that fertilized the seed which Keller's book had sown in their minds and imaginations.

In the following year, when they had been repatriated after four months in captivity, de Mun and La Tour du Pin took part in the siege of Paris. The city was in the hands of the Commune. One day when de Mun was accompanying his general to an advanced post, a group of soldiers passed them, carrying a man covered in blood. The general asked who it was. "It's an insurgent", the soldiers answered. And then the dying man, lifting himself with a supreme effort on the stretcher, pointed a naked and accusing arm at the officers and muttered faintly, "Les insurgés, c'est vous." De Mun never forgot this incident: it was a moment of revelation to him. As he noted in his memoirs: "Between these rebels and the legal society of which we were the defenders, it seemed that there was a chasm."[1]

When the siege of Paris was over, the two officers asked themselves what they could do to bridge this chasm. They consulted Louis Veuillot and Mgr Dupanloup, but received no encouragement from either. Then in the autumn of 1871 someone told them about a Young Workers' Club that had been started by the Brothers of St Vincent de Paul and was now in danger of extinction.[2] They went to see Maurice Maignen, the saintly lay brother who was responsible for it. As he talked to de Mun, he pointed out of the window to the ruins of the Tuileries, the imperial palace that had been burned to the ground during the Commune. "Who is responsible for that?" Maignen asked with animation, and then gave his answer:

[1] See Rollet, op. cit., p. 13.   [2] See p. 67 above.

It is not the people, the real people, who work and suffer. The criminals who burned Paris were not those people ... No: the guilty men, the really guilty men, *c'est vous* ... I mean the rich, the great, the fortunate who amused themselves within those ruined walls, who pass by the people, without knowing them, without seeing them, with no feeling for their souls, their needs, or their sufferings ... I live with them, and I can tell you on their behalf, they do not hate you, they are as ignorant of you as you are of them. Go to them with an open heart and an outstretched hand, and you will find that they understand you.[1]

As a result of this encounter, de Mun, La Tour du Pin, and some of their friends formed a "Committee for the foundation of Workingmen's Clubs in Paris". Their first act was to launch an "appeal to men of goodwill", which began: "The labour problem is at the present hour no longer a problem to be discussed ... it must be solved. ... The men of the privileged classes have duties they must fulfil with regard to their brothers, the workers: while society has a right to defend itself with arms in hand, it knows that shot and shell do not cure. Something else is needed."[2]

The first club they opened was in Belleville, the most squalid working-class district in Paris. It had been a stronghold of the proletarian revolution, where the fighting had been fiercest during the Commune. It was only a few minutes' walk from where Archbishop Darboy's blood had been shed. The enterprise met with success, and the promoters were soon asked to start clubs in Lyons and elsewhere. By 1875 the association had 150 clubs with 18,000 members, and it continued to expand. In 1884 it had 50,000 members.

De Mun as secretary-general toured the length and breadth of France, arousing enthusiasm by his fiery eloquence, his fine presence, and his obvious enthusiasm. He was still an officer in the army and wore uniform. The anti-clerical press complained

---

[1] See Rollet, op. cit., p. 15.   [2] Ibid., p. 16; Hoog, op. cit., pp. 16f.

that the Minister of War had no business to allow a captain of cavalry to engage in such activities. Eventually de Mun had to choose between his military career and the work of the association, and he decided to give himself entirely to the latter.

Although this Association of Workingmen's Clubs made a considerable impression and was highly creditable to those who promoted it, its importance must not be exaggerated. As a contribution to social catholicism it had serious limitations. While de Mun and his collaborators intended to avoid mere paternalism and the patronizing attitude that had been too characteristic of the conservative catholics, they were all the same apostles of the Counter-Revolution, and they were royalists who were opposed to the republican régime. La Tour du Pin refused to abandon his royalism even when in the 1890s Leo XIII directed the French catholics to rally to the Republic. De Mun by then had become more realistic. But their vaunted attachment to the doctrines of the Syllabus was bound to alienate both the liberal intelligentsia and the élite of the workers. At the same time, the clergy were hostile to the movement because it was not geared in with the parochial system and was not under their control. The government was naturally hostile because of the royalism of the promoters.

In any case, these workingmen's clubs were only in a restricted sense reaching the working class. The workers who joined the clubs were drawn not from large industrial concerns nor from agriculture, but rather from the more backward and unenterprising types of urban worker—shop assistants, caretakers, vergers, and the like. Though it is true that the association was run by laymen, by army officers and men of that class, it gave practically no responsibility to the workers themselves, and its ethos was moralizing and pietistic.[1] It probably did more to disturb the consciences of employers than to engage the interest of the working class. Perhaps its chief effect was to convince

[1] Cp. Dansette, op. cit., i, 342.

de Mun that other kinds of social catholic action were called for, if the problem he had set out to tackle was really to be solved. In particular, he came to see the need for political action.

He was elected a member of the Chamber of Deputies in 1876, where for the rest of his life he played a prominent part. Much of his energy and eloquence naturally went into the defence of the Church of France against the attacks of the anti-clericals which were now gathering momentum and would issue in the disestablishment of the Church in 1905. But all the way through those heated controversies, de Mun was also an outspoken and persistent advocate of social reform. He sat with a small group of like-minded deputies on the right, who, however much they might differ from the socialists in principle, often joined hands with them in practice in attacking the economic liberalism which was still prevalent in the French parliament. De Mun continued to maintain his connection with the workingmen's clubs, and especially with a council of studies, a kind of research group, which had arisen out of that movement. With its help he was able to make sure that he knew what he was talking about when he spoke on social questions.

Among the measures for which he pressed was a shorter working day. Personally he stood for an eight-hour day, but he saw that in the circumstances of the time it was unrealistic to hope for the passage of so progressive a measure at once. Not until 1900 did the French Parliament accept a measure enforcing an eleven-hour day, which was reduced to ten hours four years later. In this as in other respects, de Mun was in advance of most reformers. Also, against liberal opposition he campaigned for a shorter working day for women. He insisted that industry was made for man, not man for industry. He upheld the workers' right to create associations. He also urged that the responsibility of employers for accidents to the workers should be recognized. Though de Mun was left without the support of the Church and of the royalist party and was a lonely enough figure in his fight for social justice, his persistence enabled him to play a significant, and sometimes a leading part, in the fight for humane legislation.

While de Mun was the orator of this group of social catholics, La Tour du Pin was the intellectual leader.[1] He resigned his commission in the army in 1881, and henceforth gave his whole time to social studies. He asked himself what social structures would give dignity and security to the workers. He contrasted the individualism of liberal capitalism, which left each man to struggle for himself without any defence against the pitiless law of supply and demand, with the pre-revolutionary corporations. They had bound the workers in each trade and profession in an association that gave them a status in their employment and was concerned with their human interests as well as with their technical skill. When the conservative social catholics proclaimed the cause of the Counter-Revolution, they were not being blindly reactionary. They saw that the French Revolution had destroyed the ancient corporations without replacing them by anything better: it had become the parent of an inhuman, individualistic system, and the results had been deplorable. La Tour du Pin wanted to revive the corporative system in a form that was adapted to the new conditions of industry. Armed with this plan, he believed that he had a positive alternative to both *laissez-faire* capitalism and State socialism, and from now onwards this idea was canvassed and taken up by many conservative social catholics.

The third important member of this group was Léon Harmel (1829–1915).[2] He went further than de Mun and La Tour du Pin, both in theory and in practice. He wanted to give the workers genuine responsibility and to make them co-partners in industry. De Mun and La Tour du Pin, as we saw, were born aristocrats. Despite their sincere concern for the welfare of the workers, they

---

[1] See Marquis de la Tour du Pin, *Vers un ordre social chrétien: jalons de route, 1882–1907* (1929).

[2] See Georges Guitton, s.j., *Léon Harmel, 1829–1915*, 2 vols. (1927).

remained believers in a social hierarchy. It was the duty of the upper classes to serve the people and to improve their lot, but they had no sympathy with anything approaching an egalitarian democracy. Harmel, though he was older than de Mun, stands nearer to the Christian democrats who came to the fore in France towards the end of the century. He traverses the line that separates the social catholics of the right and of the left.

Harmel was an employer, an industrialist, a "patron", by inheritance and upbringing. He succeeded his father in the ownership and management of a spinning factory at Val-des-Bois, near Rheims. He was a man of intense, simple, mystical faith, who had contemplated becoming a priest. Instead, he became a tertiary of St Francis and devoted his life to a lay apostolate in the sphere which providence had assigned to him.

At Val-des-Bois the whole working community was developed as a model Christian township. It was a worshipping as well as a working community, an imaginative attempt to establish a catholic industrial democracy in practice and to work out a pattern of social relations that might be followed elsewhere. Harmel's formula was that he wanted the welfare of the workers to be achieved *by* themselves so far as possible, never *without* them, and *a fortiori* never *in spite of* them. The whole community was organized as a responsible, interdependent family, but not as a family in the old paternalistic sense. Harmel's principle was co-partnership, not "patronage".

Each worker had a detached house of his own with a garden. There were a system of family allowances (an idea Harmel derived from Le Play), which the representatives of the workers themselves controlled, a free medical service, and assistance for the sick and aged. The workers could get 4% interest on their savings, and there was a fortnightly meeting of their elected representatives to consider the business of the factory, such as safety measures against accidents, and indeed every aspect of the enterprise. Strikes were unknown at Val-des-Bois.

Harmel was an enthusiast with a sense of mission. He believed that he had discovered and proved in experience what was the key to the problem of industrial relations and a new social order. He could testify—and he travelled about testifying—to other employers that the more they gave the workers a share in authority, the more they would secure their trust and devotion. He could not make out why, when he visited other catholic employers and tried to win them to the adoption of his methods, he did not get from them an eager response.

He therefore conceived the idea of taking a group of industrialists to Rome to be received by Pope Leo XIII, with the double object of winning the employers to his ideas and of getting the pope to sanction and encourage them. He was more successful in the latter than in the former object. In 1885 100 employers went with him on pilgrimage to Rome. The pope was favourably impressed and invited them to come again. In 1887 1,800 went of whom the majority this time were workers. In 1889 10,000 went. These pilgrimages were one of the stimuli that led to the promulgation of Leo's encyclical *Rerum novarum* in 1891, which was to be a turning-point in the development of social catholicism in France and elsewhere. The practical embodiment at Val-des-Bois of the doctrine that Leo was thinking of promulgating seemed to provide him with concrete evidence that catholicism had got an answer to the industrial problem.

However, what most contributed to the preparation of the encyclical was the so-called Fribourg Union. This was a hand-picked group of social catholic leaders from France, Germany, Austria, Italy, Belgium, and Switzerland, which met annually for a week at Fribourg to study together in a systematic way what was involved in the idea of a Christian social order. These meetings, which were carefully serviced by plenty of home-work, were held from 1884 to 1891. Most of the participants were laymen, but the meetings were presided over by Mgr Gaspar Mermillod (1824–92), a radically minded prelate, who had been appointed Bishop of Geneva but had been exiled by the Swiss government and had subsequently become Bishop of Fribourg. In 1869 he had caused a scandal in Paris by a sermon in which he had contrasted the condition of the poor with that of the wealthy.[1]

Mermillod was in close touch with Rome and with Leo XIII, who made him a cardinal in 1890, and he communicated to the Vatican reports on the deliberations of the Fribourg Union. The aim of this group was to harvest the fruits of social catholic thought and experience in different countries and even to elaborate an international legislation based on a charter for industry. It was a corporative régime that they were led to desiderate, one that would co-ordinate and safeguard the interests of all who were engaged in different kinds of work. But they were not afraid of State intervention. On the contrary, they held that it was the office of the State to encourage the growth of corporations and to supervise and harmonize their activities. At first, the Fribourg Union stood for mixed corporations, that is, for syndicates in which employers and employees would be united, but they came to realize that this would be unrealistic and that employers and workers must have their separate associations, though they also made provisions which would bring them together for purposes of negotiation and arbitration. "Association" was their watchword which they contrasted with the *laissez-faire* individualism of the liberals.

The Fribourg Union affirmed man's right to work and to receive a living wage, and wanted to see an international agreement about this. It also advocated the insurance of workers against sickness, accidents, and unemployment. In 1888 Leo XIII received in audience nine of its members, discussed with them at length their proposals, and asked them to prepare a full-scale memorandum for his use. It was this memorandum that formed the basis of the encyclical *Rerum novarum*, "On the Condition of

[1] See Dansette, op. cit., i, 340.

the Workers", which the pope had had in mind for several years as part of his desire to bring about a reconciliation between the Church and modern society. Leo was a great promulgator of encyclicals. He felt the need to restate and to reinterpret the whole body of catholic teaching, and also he wanted the Church to become more outward-looking. He wanted to change the inward-looking, citadel mentality that Pius IX had fostered in the Church. In 1893, for instance, Leo said to one of the French bishops:

> Tell your priests not to shut themselves up within the walls of their church or their presbytery, but to go to the people and to concern themselves wholeheartedly with the workers, the poor, and the men of the lower classes. In our time above all, it is necessary to combat their prejudices and to bridge the abyss between the priest and the people.[1]

Much of the *Rerum novarum* now seems commonplace. Henry Scott Holland said that it was "the voice of some old-world life, faint and ghostly, speaking in some antique tongue of things long ago".[2] But to catholics it was far from being commonplace when it was promulgated. It should be seen against the background of indifference to the social problem that was still generally current in French catholicism. It had a truly epoch-making effect in driving home the idea that catholics must have a social conscience and above all that they must actively concern themselves with the condition of the workers. It is a very long document, and I can quote only one paragraph here:

> Some opportune remedy must be found quickly for the misery and wretchedness pressing so unjustly on the majority of the working class: for the ancient working-men's guilds were abolished in the last century, and no other protective organization took their

[1] See Brugerette, op. cit., ii, 377.
[2] See C. E. Hudson and M. B. Reckitt, *The Church and the World* (1940), iii, 143.

place. Public institutions and the laws set aside the ancient religion. Hence by degrees it has come to pass that working-men have been surrendered, isolated and helpless, to the hard-heartedness of employers and the greed of unchecked competition. The mischief has been increased by rapacious usury, which, although more than once condemned by the Church, is nevertheless, under a different guise, but with the like injustice, still practised by covetous and grasping men. To this must be added that the hiring of labour and the conduct of trade are concentrated in the hands of comparatively few; so that a small number of very rich men have been able to lay upon the teeming masses of the labouring poor a yoke little better than that of slavery itself.[1]

We can catch here a good many echoes of what the leading social catholics had been saying. On its negative side the encyclical was a sharp attack on unrestricted capitalism and individualistic liberalism as well as on revolutionary socialism. On the positive side, it declared the right to private property to be an inalienable human right, that is, a right for all men. It asserted that the family is the primary social unit, prior to the State. At the same time, it approved action by the State to safeguard the spiritual and material interests of the working classes. Its most striking pronouncement was to the effect that the obligation to pay the workers a living wage must not be subordinated to the pressure of so-called economic laws. The encyclical also justified the workers' right to form associations, and it encouraged the formation of catholic trade unions and workers' organizations.

The encyclical was naturally welcomed enthusiastically by those who were already social catholics and it made a considerable impression in other circles. So we find Albert de Mun saying in a speech at Lille in June 1892:

Do you remember the tremendous surprise the encyclical caused to all who like to look on the Church as only a sort of gendarme in

[1] For an English translation of the encyclical, see S. Z. Ehler and J. B. Morrall, *Church and State through the Centuries* (1954), pp. 324–55.

the service of *bourgeois* society, and to all the comfortably-off who
were scandalized when they heard the highest authority in the
world sanction ideas and doctrines which hitherto they had
regarded as fatally subversive?—and then the even greater emotion
that was caused among all the workers, the men of the people, who
for so long had been repeatedly told that they could expect nothing
from Rome but an arm raised to condemn them, and behold instead they suddenly saw a fatherly hand stretched out to bless
them?[1]

All in all, the encyclical provided a charter for social
catholic thought and action, and in France it may be said to have
set in motion the new phase of social catholicism that was known
as "Christian Democracy". It was just about this time that Leo
XIII also told the French catholics to abandon their royalism and
to rally to the Republic. In both cases his directives were coldly
received—and often ignored—by the older conservative catholics. But they released a wave of social and political ardour
among the young, especially in a new generation of clergy and
seminarists. It was from these that there arose the so-called *abbés
démocrates*, which might be translated "radical parsons".

Whereas from 1870 to 1890 the principal social catholics in
France had been laymen, in the 1890s when the Christian
democrats came to the front it was priests who were most
prominent. The *abbés démocrates* were outspoken orators and
journalists and inspirers of good works, who vigorously took
up the cause of the workers, attacked the capitalist system, and
were flamboyantly republican and democratic. There were many
such priests and they produced a whole crop of newspapers and
journals. They were also much in evidence at the congresses for
workers and at conferences for the clergy which were organized
at this time. We can look at only two or three examples of the
type.

[1] See Hoog, op. cit., p. 50.

There was Paul Naudet (1859–1929), who began his ministry in Bordeaux. In Lent 1891, when he was preaching a course of sermons, he was suddenly struck by the idea that the Church was really empty, although it was apparently crowded with a congregation of devout women. But he was thinking of the dock-workers and their comrades who were gathered outside in the inns or perhaps listening to a socialist speaker in some back room. He felt he could not go on as he was: he must find a way of meeting the workers and of carrying the Gospel to them. Then and there, he vowed that he would devote the rest of his life to an apostolate to the people. And he proceeded to do so.

Not only did he build up workers' clubs in Bordeaux. He travelled all over France addressing meetings and conferences. He founded a paper, *La Justice sociale*, as an organ of catholic democracy (he was also for a time on the staff of *Le Monde*). Leo XIII sent him a message of approval and encouragement. "It is chiefly to intellectuals that we address ourselves", wrote Naudet in *La Justice sociale*. "To sow ideas in that fertile field is to prepare for the future a rich harvest."[1]

In addition to radical social teaching, Naudet accepted the critical view of the Bible which was beginning to be disseminated by Abbé Loisy, and he made light of Loisy's condemnation when *L'Évangile et l'Église* was put on the Index. In spite of this, Leo XIII, in the last year of his pontificate, received Naudet in audience and again gave him his blessing. But during the pontificate of Pius X he ran into trouble as did the other *abbés démocrates*. Not only did Naudet maintain his sympathy with doctrinal modernism, but he defended the policy of the French Republic in disestablishing the Church, a policy that was anathema to Pius X, who would not even allow the French bishops to accept the Law of Separation, which they were prepared to do when it

[1] See Emmanuel Barbier, *Histoire du catholicisme libéral et du catholicisme social en France* (Bordeaux, 1924), iii, 439.

was a *fait accompli*. In 1908 after Pius X's condemnation of modernism, *La Justice sociale* was suppressed first by the French hierarchy and then by the Holy Office and Naudet, although he made an act of submission, was forbidden to write any more.

Pierre Dabry (1864–1916) was a powerful personality and a natural leader of men. He ran a paper of his own which was even more radical than Naudet's, and more critical of conservative catholicism. He was condemned at the same time as Naudet. Two years later he broke away from the Church, and died in penury during the first world war.

Perhaps the most attractive of the *abbés démocrates* was Jules Lemire (1853–1928), a native of Hazebrouck in French Flanders, a saintly and most engaging personality. He was ordained in 1878 and for fifteen years taught in a seminary. During this time he wrote a book on *Cardinal Manning and his social action*. He looked upon Manning as in some sense his spiritual father, though he appears to have met him only once, in 1888. In 1893 Lemire was elected as a republican deputy and held his seat for the remaining thirty-five years of his life—despite all the controversies in which he was engaged and the constant attacks of the conservative catholic press.

He was a man of the people, and he kept the affection and loyalty of the workers all his life. He lived in great simplicity and contributed effectively to the passage of many social reforms. In particular, he was responsible for a scheme to enable every working man to have a garden of his own. In his pressure for reforms, he was persistent and indefatigable, but never fanatical. Because of his integrity he was highly esteemed in Parliament, even by the anti-clericals, and was in the end elected Vice-President of the Chamber of Deputies.

In the elections of 1906 the Archbishop of Cambrai forbade Lemire to seek re-election on the ground that a Congregation in Rome had directed that priests should not offer themselves for election without the consent of the Ordinary. But a note was communicated to Lemire and to another *abbé démocrate* deputy by the papal nuncio in Paris to the effect that the directive did not apply to deputies who were seeking *re*-election. Lemire was thus able to withstand his bishop's attempt to seal him off in a country parish.

In 1910 he scandalized the conservatives, even more than he had done before, by taking a seat on the extreme left of the Chamber and by associating more closely than before with the republican deputies. The integrist catholics were now with the complaisance of Pius X hunting down every species of liberal catholicism, and in the end they succeeded in getting Lemire condemned. In January 1914 he was prohibited from saying mass. But after the death of Pius X, Benedict XV lifted the suspension, and he was not put under ecclesiastical discipline again.

As an example of his style, here is the opening paragraph of an address on "The Present Duties of the Clergy" which he gave in 1902 in the diocese of Tarentaise at the bishop's request. (The bishop, Mgr Lacroix, was associated with the modernists.)

I come to you, gentlemen, as the explorer of a world which you can hardly be said to frequent, the political world. I have been in this world for as long as ten years. I will gladly stay there. I do not want to say anything ill of it. To do so would be to condemn myself. I have another reason for speaking well of it. Too many French catholics live in their country like the Hebrews in Egypt— like exiles in the interior. Those of them, whether priests or laymen, who are sent by universal suffrage as elected representatives and into the thick of society, ought not to return with empty hands or with discouraging words, but like the messengers of Moses on their return from Canaan, with fine grapes on their shoulders and with alluring descriptions of the promised land.[1]

[1] Lemire, *Les Devoirs actuels du Clergé* (1903), p, 5.

These are but a few examples of the Christian democrat priests who flourished in the latter part of Leo XIII's pontificate but were suppressed by his successor.

The other group of social catholics of the left which belongs to this period and which deserves separate consideration is the Sillon. M. Dansette describes it as "the finest religious movement among youth that France has ever known".[1] The Sillon, which means the Furrow, was initiated by a young catholic layman, named Marc Sangnier (1873-1950).[2] He came of a prosperous and cultured family, and was educated at the Collège Stanislaus and the École Polytechnique—the equivalent of Winchester and New College. From his earliest years he acquired a magnetic influence over his companions. In 1893 at the Collège Stanislaus with some other ardent young catholics he formed a group or cell which aimed at discovering how they could devote themselves as catholics to the regeneration of their country.

As early as 1885, when he made his first communion, Sangnier had written:

What then? Because in our earliest years we have seen the religious orders exiled, and Christian schools closed, because we have seen our fathers discouraged and full of lassitude, is then everything lost? Are we going to despair of the future? Or may it not be that a new era is opening, an era of Christian salvation and renewal, of which we have perceived the dawn in our college retreat. . . .[3]

It was one of Sangnier's collaborators, Paul Renaudin, with whom he had been at school, who actually founded the journal, the *Sillon*. He was then a student at the Institut Catholique in Paris. The opening article was an address to his fellow students:

Let our first word, on the threshold of this review, be an appeal to those to whom it wants to open its pages and its heart, to our

[1] Dansette, op. cit., ii, 288.
[2] On Sangnier, see Dansette, ibid., ii, 272-88.
[3] See Lecanuet, *La Vie de l'Église sous Léon XIII* (1930), p. 678.

brothers who are just coming of age. . . . Never, never perhaps was there a time when it is more difficult to embark on life than it is to-day. . . . What solution can be given to the problem of life? . . . The old century, weary of its negations and its doubts, but too discouraged to pull itself together and renew its efforts, turns to us anxiously, as if to ask us to restore the ruins it has made . . .[1]

It was in this atmosphere of youthful idealism and missionary fervour that the *Sillon* was born. These young men were determined to take their faith outside the Church, to meet unbelievers on their own ground, and to challenge them with the idea of a Christian democracy. They had no use for the backward-looking royalism and conservatism of their elders.

At an early stage they realized that a democracy, more than any other kind of polity, requires citizens who are educated into a sense of civic responsibility. Moreover, they saw that it was not enough to reject the idea of an aristocracy or of a plutocracy as a ruling class. In a democracy leadership is still needed. The Sillonists aimed—possibly with a touch of priggishness—at contributing to the formation of an élite that would give a lead and be a creative minority, not only in colleges, but among the workers, in the army, in the professions, and in politics. They wanted to prepare themselves to become part of this élite.

The movement spread. Groups of Sillonists were formed in many places. The members were not encouraged to suppose that they had all the answers, but rather that they were called to a far-reaching task that demanded careful study and training, before they could be qualified to play a part in public life. Their mission was to show how men could be *both* convinced and practising catholics *and* wholehearted democratic republicans. By 1905 there were 200 Sillonist study groups. From 1899 onwards they had held regular national conferences.

[1] Ibid., p. 679.

In the last years of Leo XIII and the early years of Pius X the Sillon was encouraged by the Holy See, as well as by most of the French bishops who could hardly fail to approve the ardent devotion of this élite of young catholics or to withstand the fascination of Marc Sangnier himself. In 1901 Leo XIII directed the nuncio in Paris to decorate him with the cross of the Knights of St Gregory the Great. In 1902 Cardinal Richard, the Archbishop of Paris, blessed the new headquarters of the Sillon. In 1903 and again in 1904, Sangnier and some Sillonists were received in audience by Pius X who showed them all benevolence. On the second occasion the Swiss Guard at the Vatican was replaced during the audience by the Jeune Garde of the Sillonists in their black and white uniform, which was an unheard-of privilege. In December 1904 Sangnier was invited to be one of the speakers at the World Marial Congress in Rome. Again, early in 1905 Cardinal Richard presided at a mass for the Sillon in Saint-Sulpice, and read a letter from the Cardinal Secretary of State (Merry del Val) in which he said that the pope was very pleased that the Archbishop of Paris was showing so much favour to the young people of the Sillon.[1]

But from this time the clouds of ecclesiastical disapproval began to gather round them, and difficulties increased. Sangnier was a somewhat autocratic leader, and there were groups that broke away from the main body and so caused dissension. More serious were the virulent attacks on the movement that were made by the ultramontane press in France, which was relentlessly pursuing every attempt to bring about a reconciliation between the Church and contemporary society, after the example of Louis Veuillot in the previous century.

One instance—among many that might be cited—of the attacks that were made on the Sillon will suffice. In 1906 the journal *Le Jaune* contained this paragraph:

[1] See Maurice Clément, *Vie du Cardinal Richard* (1924), pp. 308f.

It is more than hate, it is *contempt* that the Sillon must inspire in those whose consciences are rightly informed. If I had to choose between the most extreme of the anarchists, between the most depraved of the socialists, and the best of the sillonists, my choice would at once be made, for the sillonist has the soul of a traitor and the instincts of treachery.[1]

The Sillon maintained that, while in matters of faith it was bound to be submissive to ecclesiastical authority, in politics it was free to pursue its own course, and by now the young men who had enlisted in the Sillon were old enough to engage in political action themselves. In 1906, when the Bishop of Quimper forbade priests and seminarists to attend a congress at which Sangnier was to speak, he made the following provocative declaration:

We are republicans and democrats. It matters little to us that the Bishop of Quimper differs from us in his political and social opinions. From the religious point of view, we are respectful and submissive sons, but . . . it is not for cardinals and bishops to lay down our political and social tactics. We incline before religious authority in so far as it is religious authority, but we intend to be free in our actions.[2]

Sangnier held that, while the members of the Sillon were sincerely and devoutly catholic, it was a lay movement which was not subject to direction or control by the bishops and parish priests. From now on, one bishop after another withdrew his support from the Sillon. Sangnier meanwhile, believing that he could still depend on the support of the pope, did not take the episcopal condemnations very seriously and went ahead with his plans for political activity. His opponents were still more enraged when he proposed to enlarge the Sillon so as to make possible collaboration with non-catholics in the pursuit of its social and political aims.

[1] See Louis Cousin, *Le Sillon et les Catholiques* (1909), p. 2.
[2] See Barbier, op. cit., iv, 436f.

Pressure was now being brought on the Holy See to condemn the movement, pressure with which the *Action française* had much to do and which the Jesuits certainly did nothing to oppose, since they had their own rival non-democratic movement for catholic youth in France. In any case the integrists were now dominant in the Vatican and it would be only a matter of time before the fate of the Sillon was sealed. A handful, but only a handful, of bishops, at the instigation of Mgr Mignot, Archbishop of Albi, who had already compromised himself by pleading for the doctrinal modernists, defended the Sillon and tried to prevent its condemnation at Rome, but without success.

On 25 August 1910 Pius X addressed a long letter to the cardinals, archbishops, and bishops of France in which he condemned the Sillon and indeed the whole movement of Christian democracy. I will translate a few paragraphs:

> The claim of the Sillon to evade the direction of ecclesiastical authority must be severely reproved. The leaders of the Sillon, in fact, allege that they are operating on a territory which is not that of the Church; that they are pursuing only the interests of the temporal order and not that of the spiritual order; that the Sillonist is simply a catholic committed to the cause of the working classes, to the tasks of democracy, who draws from the practice of his faith energy for his devotion; that, no more and no less than catholic artisans, labourers, economists, and politicians, he is subject to the rules of the morality which is common to all, without involving, any more or less than they do, in any special manner, ecclesiastical authority.
>
> The answer to these subterfuges is only too easy. Who in fact will believe that the catholic Sillonist, and the priests and seminarists who are enrolled in their ranks, have in view, in their social action, only the temporal interests of the working classes? It would, we think, be an insult to them to maintain that this is so. The truth is that the leaders of the Sillon declare themselves to be indomitable idealists, that they claim to raise the working classes by raising first the human conscience, that they have a social doctrine and

philosophical and religious principles for the reconstruction of society on a new plan, that they have a special conception of human dignity, of liberty, of justice and of fraternity, and that, in order to justify their social dreams, they appeal to the Gospel, interpreted in their own manner, and, what is still more grave, to a disfigured and diminished Christ . . .

If their doctrine were free from error, it would in any case have been a very serious failure in catholic discipline to withdraw obstinately from the direction of those who have received from heaven the mission to guide individuals and societies in the right way. . . . But the evil goes deeper . . . the Sillon, carried away by a misconceived love of the weak, has fallen into error.

In fact, the Sillon proposes the restoration and regeneration of the working classes. But, as regards this, the principles of catholic doctrine are fixed, and the history of Christian civilization is there to attest their beneficial results.[1]

And so on. The pope's doctrine was purely traditional and conservative, as might have been expected by anyone who had taken to heart the encyclical which Pius X had addressed to the Italian Christian democrats in 1903. There he had said:

It is in conformity with the order established by God that there shall be in human society princes and subjects, capitalists and proletarians, rich and poor, the learned and the ignorant, nobles and plebeians, who, all united by a bond of love, ought to help one another mutually to attain their last end in heaven, and on earth their material and moral well-being . . . Catholic writers, in supporting the cause of the proletarians and the poor, must be careful not to use a language that can inspire in the people an aversion from the upper classes of society. Let them not speak of claims and of justice when charity alone is in question.[2]

It must be confessed that Leo XIII, along with his encouragement to Christian democracy, had also on occasion said things

---

[1] See Albert Houtin, *Histoire du Modernisme Catholique* (1913), pp. 293f.
[2] See Alfred Loisy, *L'Église et la France* (1925), pp. 90f.

rather like that. At all events, all the new currents of social catholic thought and action that had been inspired by Leo's goodwill, now found themselves frustrated and condemned. When Pius X condemned the Sillon so ruthlessly in 1910, M. Loisy said to his friends: "The Roman Church has no heart."[1] It seemed to him to be the most odious of all Pius X's acts. In the condemnation of doctrinal modernism the pope had had the excuse he was dealing with what, by traditional standards of orthodoxy, was manifestly a heresy. In the condemnation of the Sillon no such issue was involved. What was at issue was the possibility of catholics' engaging in social and political action without being subjected to the control and direction of the ecclesiastical hierarchy.

The Sillon had to be dissolved, for very few of the members were willing to join groups that would be directly subject to the bishops, which is what the pope had demanded. Sangnier and his collaborators had to make a humble submission to the papal ruling, and to give up their attempt to serve the cause of Christian democracy. Sangnier himself did indeed continue to serve the democratic cause, but now on a purely political basis.[2]

Although at the turn of the century it had looked as if there was a good prospect in France that the social catholicism of the left might be going to make a real impact on the political world and on industrial society, the prospect was never so bright as it seemed. Only a minority of catholics was really concerned, and they were for the most part young. Then, French catholicism continued to be agitated and weakened by internecine quarrels; the attitude of the majority of catholics in the Dreyfus affair, and in the disputes that led up to the separation of Church and State, was not calculated to warrant the hope that the Church was really favourable to social progress or that it had learned anything from its mistakes in the nineteenth century. Again, Pius X

[1] Loisy, *Mémoires* (1931), ii, 363.
[2] See M. D. Petre, *Modernism: its failure and its fruits* (1918), pp. 239f.

for all his personal piety was thoroughly reactionary in his ecclesiastical policies, and he was determined to stamp out by all the means in his power everything that savoured of either doctrinal or social modernism. And all the time a savage campaign was being carried on in the French Church by the heirs of Louis Veuillot against any innovators who would not toe a rigidly ultramontane line.

Thus the dice were heavily loaded against the young social catholics of the Sillon. They were up against forces which no amount of generous idealism or ardent devotion or realistic intelligence—and they had plenty of these qualities—could overcome. French society as a whole, despite their aspirations, continued to be split between clericalism and anti-clericalism, and the day had not yet come when any substantial reconciliation or reorientation was possible. The most that can be said is that seeds were sown at this time that were to bear fruit in later manifestations of Christian democracy and catholic action. Pius X had succeeded in putting the clock back with a vengeance.

7

Belgium: 1870-1920[1]

At the beginning of the 1870s there was a period of industrial expansion and prosperity in Belgium. Wages increased and the hardships of the workers were to some extent eased. This was all very well, but the workers would be all the more discontented if there were a recession and they had to forgo the modest advances that had taken place in their standard of living. In fact, from 1873 onwards there was a recession. Unemployment became more and more serious and wages were continually reduced. Here is a statement made by a worker at this time which speaks for itself.

I am a working-man employed now in the phosphate quarries. I earn 2.50 fr. a day and I have a boy who works with me and gets 1.75 fr. a day. . . . We are a family of seven: myself, my wife, and five children, and the rent of the house is 11 fr., and we have to buy everything we need to live. I dare say that for seven or eight years I have run up many debts; all the same, I claim that I am a respectable working-man and I do not frequent the cabarets. I am a good father to my family, I am very fond of my children, I have plenty of pluck, I never lose a day's work by my own fault, for I have never been a drunkard. But hardship makes life burdensome to me. I gladly go on living, however, in order to bring up my children,

[1] For this period, see Rudolf Rezsohazy, *Origines et formation du catholicisme social en Belgique, 1842-1909*; Maurice Vaussard, *Histoire de la démocratie chrétienne: France, Belgique, Italie*; Henri Haag on "The Catholic Movement in Belgium, 1789-1950" in *Church and Society*, ed. J. N. Moody, pp. 279-324.

but they have to run around with no shoes or stockings; none of us has any bedding, how are we to face the winter which is about to come on us?[1]

Thousands of workers could have made statements like this. It was now only the older workers who were illiterate. Education was producing its effects, and the younger workers were less resigned to their lot than their fathers had been. They were becoming competent to speak for themselves and to organize themselves.

In the 1880s economic conditions continued to deteriorate until they produced a crisis in March 1886. It was started by an anarchist group in Liège which invited workers to a meeting to commemorate the fifteenth anniversary of the Paris Commune. This set off a series of strikes which issued in rioting and indeed in a widespread insurrection. The army was called out, blood was shed, and the *bourgeoisie* was thoroughly scared. The emergency went on for some weeks.

The importance of this event in the present connection is that it rudely awakened the intellectuals and the well-to-do to the wretched condition of the working class. Many members of the younger generation realized for the first time that they must do something about the social problem. This was especially true of the catholics. They realized now from what they heard of other countries that Belgium was extremely backward in its social legislation. They heard of Mgr Ketteler's initiatives in Germany and of the formation of the centre party there, of the growth of trade unionism in England and of Cardinal Manning's sympathy with it, of the catholic working-men's clubs in France, and of the idea of a Christian corporatism which was being adumbrated by de Mun and La Tour du Pin. The Fribourg Union had begun to meet in 1884. Several of the leading social catholics in other countries had visited Belgium, and their visits had had a stimulating effect. All these circumstances, which were prior to

[1] See Rezsohazy, op. cit., p. 99.

the promulgation of the papal encyclical *Rerum novarum* in 1891, gave a stronger impetus to the incipient Christian democrat movement in Belgian catholicism.

The first sign of new activity was a congress which was held at Liège in 1886 and had been prepared for by a society known as the "Union nationale pour le redressement des griefs". The members of this society saw that the days of paternalism and "patronage" were passed. In any case, in large industries the relations between employers and workers were too impersonal and remote for charity to work in the old way. It was time to talk of justice. It had therefore been decided to call a congress to canvass this idea. In fact, a series of three congresses was held before the *Rerum novarum* was issued—in 1886, 1887, and 1890.

It was in these congresses that the newer, progressive type of social catholicism staked out its claims and won adherents. Cardinal Manning wrote a letter to the Third Congress of Liège, in which he said:

> I do not believe that it will ever be possible to establish peaceful relations between employers and workers, until it is publicly acknowledged and established that there must be a just and fitting measure that will regulate profits and wages, a measure that will govern all the free contracts between capital and labour.[1]

The reading of this letter caused a sensation among the conservative members of the congress who were still in the majority. Their leader, Charles Woeste (1837–1922)—of whom it was said that "he was interested in nothing but increasing the budget for the Churches and the State grants to the Catholic schools"—[2] expressed his great satisfaction that the congress did not go nearly so far as Cardinal Manning had done in his letter.

Nevertheless, the Christian democrats were all the time gaining ground in the catholic party. The conservatives were just

[1] Ibid., p. 106.

[2] See Michael P. Fogarty, *Christian Democracy in Western Europe, 1820–1953* (1957), p. 314.

preparing to launch a counter-offensive against their increasing influence when the encyclical *Rerum novarum* appeared which justified the state intervention and social legislation that were bugbears to the conservatives.

The progressive social catholics perceived that the workers themselves intended now to take their own cause in hand, and, if the catholics had nothing relevant to say, the socialists would carry all before them. This became clear at meetings which were arranged for working men during the catholic congresses. The workers were not disposed simply to be harangued by princes of the Church and *bourgeois* intellectuals. They wanted to speak for themselves.

In its first phase, the social catholicism that found expression in these congresses was mainly corporatist. Corporatism in Belgium was a kind of parenthesis between the old paternalism and the emergence of a full-blown Christian democratic movement. The Belgian corporatists adopted the ideas of de Mun and La Tour du Pin which reached them through the participation of their own leaders in the Fribourg Union. One of the Belgian leaders, Georges Helleputte (1852–1925), was a brother-in-law of de Mun. He went through a corporatist phase, but later became a Christian democrat.

Catholic corporatism, as we have seen before, was based on the idea that the French Revolution had done untold harm by destroying the ancient corporations or trade guilds, and by leaving the workers without any mutual support to face the hazards of *laissez-faire* capitalism. Mixed up with it was a good deal of romanticism about the Middle Ages and the *ancien régime*, but there was a valid perception that the individualism which was the creed of liberalism would never produce a tolerable social order. The corporatists held that social pacification had three necessary elements: first, the legitimate desire of the lower classes to improve their condition and to raise their status in society; second, the spirit of sacrifice in the ruling classes which would lead them voluntarily to forgo some of their privileges and material advantages; and third, patience in the workers to await these improvements without resorting to insurrection.

These thinkers envisaged corporations which would be associations composed of people in the same profession, who would combine to defend their professional dignity and interests and to seek their material and moral welfare. For this purpose they would have to be *mixed* corporations, embracing employers and employees in one organization. It seemed to the corporatists that workers' syndicates were formed for conflict and so could never bring about a reconciliation between capital and labour.

The corporations would be concerned with wage rates, with the housing of the workers, with insurance against sickness, accidents, and unemployment, with facilities for savings and credit, with technical training of the young, and with provision for recreation. Each corporation would have a patron saint, religious offices, and priestly ministrations. Religion would inculate the spirit of sacrifice and moral obligation in the employers and the spirit of patience in the workers. The workers would have a certain share in the profits. The State would intervene only to redress abuses and to give legal personality to the corporations. Eventually, the corporations would be grouped on a professional or regional basis, and should be related to one another in a national organization that would limit production and prevent competition. The corporations would send representatives to the national Parliament.

This corporatist theory did not remain purely theoretical in Belgium. A number of corporations was actually formed in the 1870s and 1880s. For example, when the catholic University of Louvain decided to build a new college, the professor of architecture was enabled to form a special guild of masons, carpenters, plumbers, painters, etc., to carry the work through. This guild was so popular and so successful that it was maintained in being afterwards. The original fourteen members in 1878 had become ninety in 1886 and over a thousand in 1893. Similar corporations were formed at Brussels, Bruges, Liège, and elsewhere. They had a limited success, but they were not sufficiently democratic in constitution to satisfy the aspirations of the workers, nor were they able to exercise any control over the economy or to secure political representation. They were in fact an ephemeral phenomenon, and should be regarded as a transitional stage between the old paternalism and the emergence of the Christian trade unions or workers' syndicates.

The encyclical *Rerum novarum* gave a great fillip to social catholic thought in Belgium. It would not be an exaggeration to say that a really profound catholic sociology was elaborated, which could offer itself as a positive alternative to both economic liberalism and socialism. Its criticism of liberalism had much in common with that of the socialists. But the socialists were secularists, whereas the social catholics, who were now calling themselves, "Christian democrats", took their stand on a Christian doctrine of man in society. So one of them, Henry Carton de Wiart (1869–1951), who had been influenced by de Mun and the Society of St Vincent de Paul, said in a book, entitled *L'action catholique des démocrates chrétiens* (1895):

> We want every man who works to be able to gain his bread in conditions that satisfy both his physical and moral needs, in conditions that satisfy his dignity, and help him to fulfil his destiny in this life and the next. We want this for every man, and particularly for the worker.[1]

The individual man could not secure this satisfaction for himself. The State had a natural right and duty to promote the common good and to this end it could intervene in private affairs. Employers who injured the welfare of the workers should be dealt with by the State as criminals were.

[1] See Rezsohazy, op. cit., p. 176.

When a poor devil steals from a rich industrialist the bread that he needs, you appeal to the State. You find the gendarme and the magistrate and bring the wretched man before a tribunal that condemns him. But when it is a case of the poor devil's being deprived of his health, of his family life, of his soul, you refuse to let the State intervene. Where is the logic?[1]

The Christian democrats thus had a doctrine which required the State to intervene through social legislation wherever that would serve the common good. They held that social legislation ought to provide for a living wage, regulate the conditions of employment, and control the economy. All the same, these social catholics were afraid of giving too much control to the State. They favoured a pluralist order in which associations, especially trade unions and co-operative societies, would have a proper autonomy. They differed from the corporatists in wanting separate associations for employers and workers to represent their divergent interests. They also pressed for the representation of the workers in Parliament by working men, and they had much to say about electoral reform and a wider suffrage.

They had no hesitation in saying that catholicism must be progressive and move with the times. If the world changes, the catholics ought not to remain immobile. Granted that their dogmas should not change, but the way of presenting them should. The Church should be always on the march. A rigid catholicism, always showing the same aspect of the truth, might correspond well enough with the *ancien régime* when change was rare and slow. Contemporary society was quite different. Events, systems, states of mind, were succeeding one another with an increasing acceleration. Catholicism must follow them and meet them where they were. So we find Jules Renkin (1862–1934), who later held government office and was one of the most dynamic social catholics, saying in 1893:

[1] Ibid., p. 177.

As a matter of fact catholicism is not at all conservative in the usual sense of the word, that is to say, a matter of routine, a defender of of what is ancient, a *laudator temporis acti*, but it is essentially progressive because it seeks the ever more perfect realization in this world of the moral law.[1]

Another of their themes was the need for an apostolate of the laity:

The apostolate of lay catholics is an absolute necessity in contemporary society. Laymen can make their way everywhere, even in *milieux* which are closed to the priest.[2]

How far, we must ask, did these Belgian Christian democrats succeed in translating their doctrine into practice and especially into social legislation?

It will be recalled that the union between the catholics and the liberals which had achieved Belgian independence in 1830 was dissolved in 1857, when the liberal party went to the country with the cry, "Down with the priests!" and won seventy seats against thirty-eight for the catholic or conservative party.[3] There followed a period during which liberal and catholic governments alternated, and there were bitter feuds between them about religious and secular education. But at length the liberals overplayed their hand. In 1884, in revulsion from a ruthless attempt on their part to secularize education, a large catholic majority was returned and it retained power for the next quarter of a century. So it transpired that, when the Christian democrats came forward with their proposals for social reform, the catholic party was firmly in power.

Consequently, the political outlook and the location of power were quite different in Belgium from what they were in France, though this is by no means to say that the Christian democrats

---

[1] Ibid., p. 199. [2] Ibid. [3] See p. 93 above.

had things all their own way. The catholic party was still predominantly conservative, in fact as well as in name. The young Christian democrats—some of whom were intellectuals, and some an élite of catholic workers—had to decide whether to form a party of their own and act independently or to enter into an alliance with an already existing party. After a little oscillation they decided to join forces with the catholic party despite its conservatism.

They therefore set about waging a campaign to convert the catholics to Christian democracy, or at least to secure a sufficient majority in the party to be able to determine its policy. They did steadily increase their influence in the party and were able to get some salutary reforms adopted. But until 1907 Charles Woeste continued to be the leader of the party and a very powerful one at that. He belonged to the old school of catholic conservatives who regarded the division between rich and poor as being providentially ordained. He refused, so long as he could, to have any Christian democrats in the government.

But throughout this period they were the driving force in the catholic party, and the conservatives could do no more than check their advance. Undoubtedly, by uniting with the catholic party the Christian democrats had to be content with many compromises and they could not get their whole programme carried out, but they were probably able to achieve more in this way than they would have been able to do if they had tried to act as an independent party.

All the time too, they were building up support in the catholic trade unions. The trade union organization, *La Ligue démocratique belge*, which in 1893 had only 70,000 members, by 1909 had 200,000 members. As regards the representation of the Christian democrats in Parliament, they had eight deputies in 1898; from 1902 onwards they had at least fifteen or twenty, so that the catholic party could not form a government without their support.

One reason why the catholic party was able to maintain a majority for so long was that there was a system of plural voting that favoured the conservatives and handicapped the socialists, and also of course handicapped the Christian democrats. It was therefore a great advantage to the cause of social reform that the Christian democrats were so strongly entrenched in the catholic party. On a long view, it was also a great asset to the catholic cause in Belgium that the Christian democrats were able to prevent the identification of catholicism with the conservative defence of privilege, and to associate it in the mind of the workers with the promotion of their interests. Catholicism acquired a new image as the inspiration of a reforming party. There was substance in the image, for the outlook of the Christian democrats did gradually permeate the whole catholic party.

The social legislation of Belgium during this period of catholic ascendancy bears comparison with that of any other country, and the Belgian social catholics had a highly creditable record of practical achievement. They had the approval of their own ecclesiastical authorities and also of the Holy See, though at first some of the bishops had been hostile to their aims. When Mgr Désiré-Joseph Mercier (1851–1926)—who was famous during the first world war as Cardinal Archbishop of Malines—came to the front of affairs, the social catholics had in him a reliable supporter. The clergy also were in sympathy with the Christian democrats and were fellow workers in the cause. A special community of priests was formed known as *Aumoniers du travail* (labour chaplains) who gave themselves entirely to an apostolate among the workers. They served the Christian trade unions, looked after workers' hostels and technical schools, and in many other ways brought the ministry of the Church into the practical service of the workers.

The Christian trade unions or syndicates were more pragmatic than ideological, reformist and not revolutionary. They were wisely led and did much to improve the status of the workers.

They also promoted a genuine working-class culture through their newspapers, courses of lectures, conferences, study circles, and social weeks (*semaines sociales*).

The first world war inevitably put social catholicism everywhere more or less in the shade for the time being, and when it was over a new phase of its history would open which lies beyond the limits of this book. But it can safely be said that by the end of the first decade of the twentieth-century social catholicism was not only an essential characteristic of the catholic party in Belgium, but that it had taken root in the life of the country as a whole. It may of course be thought that it would have been better still if the movement for the emancipation of the workers and the reform of the social order could have been a united movement instead of being split between the Christian democrats and the socialists. This question is bound up with the larger question of the desirability of having "Christian" political parties and "Christian" trade unions. It is a question that appears in a different light in Britain from what it does on the Continent.[1] In Belgium the split between the Christian democrats and the socialists was inevitable in view of the deep division in the country about religion and clericalism.

It is satisfactory to be able to conclude that, just as the Belgian catholics were among the first to make liberal political principles their own, so they were among the first to break the identification of the Church with the defence of privilege and with retrograde social policies. Christian democracy in Belgium had much in common with the empirical social democracy of the labour movement in England, but in Belgium the movement was more positively Christian; indeed it was positively catholic.

[1] On this whole subject, see Fogarty, op. cit.

8

Italy[1]

There were liberal catholics in Italy during the period of the Risorgimento which ended in 1870, though Pio Nono was gravely displeased with them, but there was nothing worth mentioning that can be reckoned as social catholicism until towards the last quarter of the century. And then Italian social catholicism was largely derivative, stimulated by the example of what was being done in France, Belgium, and Germany. But it must also be seen against its peculiar historical background.

The Revolutionary and Napoleonic wars at the beginning of the century had affected Italy politically more perhaps than any other country in Europe. "The French occupation", says J. N. Moody, "had profoundly altered Italian destiny. The instinct to hail the Corsican (i.e. Napoleon I) as one of the founders of United Italy is sound. . . . He had shaken the peninsula from its somnolence and had introduced wide social and legal changes that could be modified but not erased."[2] The awakening, however, was political: little was changed in the country's economic condition. It remained a weak and backward country, impoverished by being parcelled out into so many

[1] On social catholicism in Italy, see Maurice Vaussard, *Histoire de la démocratie chrétienne: France, Belgique, Italie*; R. A. Webster, *Christian Democracy in Italy, 1860–1960* (1961); A. C. Jemolo, *Church and State in Italy, 1850–1950* (E.T., 1960); Michael P. Fogarty, *Christian Democracy in Western Europe, 1820–1953*; L. H. Jordan, *Modernism in Italy* (1909); F. S. Nitti, *Catholic Socialism* (E.T., 1895).

[2] Moody *Church and Society*, p. 31.

states and by the power exercised over them by foreign governments.

The struggle that was to occupy the most enterprising Italians until 1870 was the struggle for independence and for unity. Little attention was paid to the need for reform and development of the national economy. It was mainly an agricultural country. Most of the people were poor, but the poverty was different from that brought about by the Industrial Revolution. Often it was worse. Especially was this so in Naples and Sicily, or the Kingdom of the Two Sicilies as they were known. Economic conditions there were as bad as in the Balkans, and human beings often had to live like animals. Even after the success of the Risorgimento there was little improvement. As late as the 1870s there was no change in the appalling way in which children were employed in the Sicilian sulphur mines.

With regard to the States of the Church, Cavour once said that the papal government was the only one in the world that did not accept the principles of reason and experience in the management of temporal affairs. The Two Sicilies were actually worse, but the clerically controlled papal states and Rome itself were notorious for their misgovernment. In Rome the contrast was glaring between the abundance of sumptuously furnished churches, grandiose palaces, convents, and other buildings devoted to religious uses—and the sordid streets and slums in which the poor had to eke out a living. It was a scandal throughout Europe, and its unpopularity on the spot was shown by the fact that in the plebiscite in 1870 which brought to an end the temporal power of the popes, there were only 46 votes cast in Rome itself and 1,461 in the papal states against the annexation to the Kingdom of Italy in comparison with respectively 40,785 and 92,896 for annexation.

Likewise in Venetia in 1871, about a third of the population were paupers. In Lombardy things were rather better. But in 1877 a commission which carried out a careful inquiry into the condition of agricultural workers reported that their housing conditions were deplorable, their food unwholesome, their drinking water putrid, and their wages ridiculous. But the commission had no idea how things could be improved. The large proprietors had no sense of social responsibility. Piedmont was the most prosperous country and the policy of free trade that had been forwarded by Cavour had a beneficial effect on the economy.

After the Union of Italy in 1870, the resources of the country as a whole were, however, still very poor, and the successors of Cavour had first to put its finances in order. In the ensuing period there were two schools of thought. One wanted to develop the internal cohesion of the country and to raise its standard of living. The other was bent on ensuring its external security and making Italy one of the Great Powers. The two aims were incompatible, and unfortunately the second prevailed, that is, a politics of prestige. The Italian government suffered from an inferiority complex. For fifty years vast sums were spent on building up a navy, while the condition of the people was neglected and the battle that ought to have been undertaken against illiteracy was disregarded. The figures for illiteracy, especially in the south, were phenomenal. In 1880 the percentage of illiterate army conscripts in Italy was 49, compared with $1\frac{1}{2}$ in Germany, 5 in Sweden, and $14\frac{1}{2}$ in France. Although compulsory education was voted in 1877, for a long time the law remained a dead letter.

What, we have to ask, did the catholics do about all this? The answer is that, so far as political action went, they did practically nothing. When the temporal power came to an end in 1870, the papacy made its restoration the only vital political issue. In this respect, Leo XIII faithfully followed Pius IX, at any rate until the last years of his pontificate. It has been estimated that Leo, the prisoner in the Vatican, issued sixty-two formal protests against past or present actions of the Italian government. Catholics were forbidden to acknowledge that the Kingdom of Italy had come to stay and they were not allowed to take part in the politics of their country. To begin with, some catholics tried to evade the papal ruling, but the Vatican tightened its prohibitions against their standing for Parliament or voting at elections, though it appears that the bulk of rural catholics did vote all the same. They had no interest in the restoration of the temporal power. That was a preoccupation of the papacy and the catholic aristocracy. The question bedevilled Italian catholicism even more than legitimism had bedevilled French catholicism.

In this respect, the accession of Pius X represented a change for the better. He had no interest in the temporal power, even if he paid lip-service to the stand that had been taken by his predecessors. He was a staunch Italian patriot, and when he was asked what he would do if the King offered to abandon Rome to him he said that he would at once reply, "Stay where you are".[1] Thus he did not want the Italian catholics to continue to live in isolation as a community apart, and from 1904 onwards he began here and there to dispense them from the prohibition against participation in politics. Unhappily he was himself so rigidly conservative that, as we shall see, he made it impossible for a promising progressive movement to develop.

As regards the beginnings of social catholicism in Italy, there were various organizations of a paternalistic kind before 1874 for the distribution of charity, the promotion of education, and the formation of youth clubs. From 1874 these and other kinds of what came to be called "catholic action" were combined in a general organization, known as the *Opera dei Congressi*. There were annual congresses with an abundance of oratory, of which Germany and Belgium had set an example. The *Opera dei Congressi* held together an extensive and varied ramification of activities, many of them local. Of course it steadfastly supported

[1] See D. A. Binchy, *Church and State in Fasçist Italy* (1941), p. 55.

the papacy and was docile to its instructions. The catholics who controlled it were strongly conservative, opposed both to liberalism and socialism. It sent representatives to congresses in other countries and to the Fribourg Union. Even before the promulgation of *Rerum novarum* there was a modest ferment of new social thought. In a retrospective review of this period, an Italian professor of ecclesiastical history wrote:

> The priests who worked in the Christian-social field prior to the encyclical *Rerum novarum* were few and far between and, apart from rare exceptions, those who did had very restricted ideas and aims. Some began to study in St Thomas the principles concerning social justice, usury, credit . . . but they forgot that principles are not the same thing as their application, and anyhow that the application of thomist principles to the most burning current issues was not to be found in the *Summa*. . . . So they delivered discourses that were excellent from a doctrinal point of view, but that had no practical result. [1]

Nevertheless, there was already among younger catholics, both clerical and lay, a yearning for bolder and more radical ideas and forms of action,[2] and the *Rerum novarum* gave them just the impetus and encouragement that they needed. It was now that the movement to be known as "Christian Democracy" got under way. Its most important thinker was Guiseppe Toniolo (1845–1918), professor of economics and law at Pisa, who had started a group for the study of catholic social teaching in 1888. Toniolo himself was a corporatist who advocated mixed corporations of masters and workmen, profit-sharing in industry, and small holdings. He had the confidence of Leo XIII and was a man of manifest piety. He was greatly respected by the younger Christian democrats who, however, were impatient of his

[1] See Vaussard, op. cit., p. 224.
[2] See G. la Piana, "A Review of Italian Modernism" (art.), *Harvard Theological Review*, October 1916, pp. 351–75.

moderation and caution. The fact that he was so widely trusted enabled him to keep the Christian democrats within the *Opera dei Congressi* although the conservatives who controlled it viewed them with considerable alarm.

Their alarm increased when a brilliant young priest, Don Romolo Murri (1870–1944), came to the front as the leader of the Christian democrats. He first became famous through a vigorous protest against the severity with which the government suppressed widespread socialist disorders that occurred all over Italy in 1898. Murri was a born leader and organizer, an aggressive propagandist and writer. He accepted the papal prohibition of standing for parliament and voting in elections, but regarded it as a provisional measure which gave catholics the opportunity to work out their social policy and to build up their political organization throughout the country with a view to entering the political field at a future date, when they would be fully prepared to set about introducing a new social order.

The young Christian democrats, led by Murri, published their programme in 1899.[1] They demanded that the State should allow full freedom to trade unions and associations. They stood for proportional representation in Parliament, for the decentralization of administration and local and regional autonomy, for a fixed minimum wage and hours of work, for sickness, accident, and old age insurance, for co-operative societies, for the establishment of a ministry of labour, for taxation reform, for extension of the franchise, for progressive disarmament, etc. This was to be the programme for a Christian social order, of which the papacy would be the natural centre.

Murri has been said, with justice, to have had much in common with both Lamennais and Marc Sangnier. Certainly he had a capacity for inspiring immense enthusiasm. A contemporary observer described Murri's following in these words:

---

[1] For full text, see Fogarty, op. cit., pp. 319f.

The Christian Democrats . . . are one of the most hopeful religious symptoms of modern Italy: for they are sincere earnest men, imbued with the desire to apply religion to life. They wish to purge the slums, to raise the downtrodden, to educate the ignorant, to bring to the masses a helpful knowledge of the social and economic principles to which the world now looks for health, and to kindle among the *élite* a sense of their responsibility. They saw the avowed Socialists doing, among the lower classes, the work that ought to be done by the followers of Jesus Christ.[1]

The programme of the young Christian democrats was hotly debated in the *Opera dei Congressi*, and caused much controversy and tension in that body. It was opposed not only by the intransigent conservatives but also by those catholics who were now disposed to collaborate with liberals in order to withstand the advance of socialism. It was also too extreme for the moderate Christian democrats, represented by Toniolo, who broke with Murri in 1903. Murri's position was complicated by the fact that he evinced keen sympathy with the doctrinal modernists and with those who were agitating for an internal reform of the Church. In December 1901 Baron von Hügel and Mgr Mignot were staying in Rome at the same time, seeking to promote the modernist cause, and among those whom they met was, as von Hügel wrote to Loisy, an "abbé démocrate, who, with the support of Cardinal Agliandi, publishes in Rome itself a paper which permits itself to use language of an astonishing freshness."[2] This was Murri.

In an encyclical of 18 January 1901 (*Graves de communi*) Leo XIII had approved the use of the expression "Christian democracy" with the proviso that it had no political implications. This could not satisfy Murri who had formed his followers into a "National Democratic League" which was independent of the hierarchy. A challenging speech which he made in August 1902 was censured by the Vatican, but he

[1] See Jordan, op. cit., p. 28.   [2] See Loisy, *Mémoires*, ii, 80.

submitted and so the crisis was deferred. In November 1902 a congress of the *Opera dei Congressi* was held at Bologna, and it was a triumphant occasion for Murri and his party. But the old guard which still had a majority on the controlling committee asserted themselves with a view to disowning the young Christian democrats. Leo was by this time very frail and disposed to leave difficult problems to be settled by his successor. A few weeks before his death on 20 July 1903 he he had received Murri in audience and given him his blessing.

The accession of Pius X brought matters to a head. He was not at all inclined to temporize and he was not going to tolerate professedly catholic movements or parties which claimed to be independent of ecclesiastical control. In 1904 therefore he dissolved the *Opera dei Congressi* and replaced it by a new organization (*Unione Popolare*) which would be controlled by the hierarchy and could not develop into, or provide a sounding board for, an autonomous political party.

Murri and his followers continued their campaign outside this new organization and still won support, but the eventual fate of the young Christian democrats or social modernists was as surely sealed as was that of the doctrinal modernists. It was only a matter of time before this intransigent and determined pope would strike his final blows. Murri did not want to leave the Church, since he would then probably lose his following: so he compromised and equivocated as long as he could. He was actually excommunicated on 22 March 1909, shortly after he had been elected to Parliament as a radical deputy. After his excommunication he still claimed to be a priest, but "those Christian democrats who neither approved his doctrinal aberrations nor imitated his defiance were forced into an unhappy silence".[1] In 1912 Murri announced his marriage, and after that he could obviously no longer carry any good catholics along with him,

[1] Binchy, op. cit., p. 63.

and in any case, so long as Pius X remained pope, there was no prospect of a revival of Christian democracy.

In an article which was published in the *Hibbert Journal* in July 1922 Murri summed up his view of the course he had followed:

It seemed to be within the scope of Modernism to take a decisive step in advance in the conception of the relations between religion and politics, between Church and State. Between 1892 and 1902, Catholic Italians, who had up till then held aloof from the public life of their country, were deeply stirred by a movement towards democracy and an emancipated culture. Its representatives at first took up Gioberti's idea, and sought to prepare the way for a triumphant return of the Church and the Papacy to their leadership in the advance of civilisation. The illusion soon vanished, and, under pressure of the suspicion and persecution of the Vatican, their second thought was to demand a clean cut between religion and politics, so as to remain firmly attached and obedient adherents of the Church as believers, while recognising no rule but that of their own conscience in political and social action.[1]

In 1914 a new period opened in which events occurred that created a more favourable atmosphere in Italy for catholic social and political action. Pope Pius X died at the beginning of the first world war, and was succeeded by Benedict XV, a comparatively liberal pope in the tradition of Leo XIII. Then, when Italy entered the war, the Italian catholics participated in it with conspicuous patriotism, and at last broke down the idea that they were an alien body within the Kingdom of Italy. They even found fault with the pope for his neutrality and appeals for peace. Further, it was now generally accepted that the restoration of the temporal power of the papacy in anything like its old form was a dead notion.

[1] Loc. cit., p. 652. Not long before his death in 1944 Murri was reconciled to the Church with the goodwill of Pope Pius XII, of whom at one time he had been a fellow student, and without being required to disavow his past social and political beliefs.

In these circumstances, a revival of the Christian democrat movement became a possibility at the end of the war, and a new leader was ready to show the way. This was Don Luigi Sturzo (1871–1959), a priest who had collaborated with Romolo Murri in the earlier phase of the movement, but had not been compromised by any flirtation with doctrinal modernism. He was a Sicilian by origin, and had had much experience of municipal administration and of the promotion of co-operative societies and trade unions. He was thus a well-seasoned man of affairs and both more patient and more of a political realist than Murri had been.

Towards the end of 1918 Sturzo judged that the time was ripe for the formation of a new party, which would have a new name "the popular party" though its policy would be similar, if less flamboyantly expressed, to that of the young Christian democrats of 1899. But it was to be a non-confessional party, i.e. not confined to catholics, and it would be free of ecclesiastical control. Benedict XV was quite willing for this. Before the party was actually launched in January 1919, Sturzo had been to see the papal secretary of state to request the pope to abolish the *non expedit*, the prohibition on catholics' taking part in elections, and he had received a private assurance that this would be done.[1] The *non expedit* was in fact abolished unostentatiously in November 1919.

The popular party at once attracted widespread support, both from groups of catholics that had previously been organized for various kind of social work and from other quarters that welcomed this new political initiative. Sturzo himself later described the sources from which the party's support was drawn in the following passage:

At the beginning of 1919 . . . there were in Italy in the hands of Social Catholics more than four thousand co-operatives, some one

[1] See L. Sturzo, *Nationalism and Internationalism* (New York, 1946), p. 114.

thousand workers' mutual aid societies, about three hundred popular banks, many professional unions (which had been confederated together in September, 1918) reaching within a short time a membership of almost eight hundred thousand (in 1920 a million, two hundred thousand). Moreover, many of the students of the secondary schools and universities had been educated for a long time in Catholic Youth clubs. They had given during the war a magnificent example of military courage and Christian virtues. They came spontaneously into the Popular Party, becoming its intellectual and moral lever, just as the working masses of the Catholic Unions, leagues and Peasant Co-operatives were its most convinced and disciplined recruits. Finally, the co-operation of the middle and intellectual classes, doctors, lawyers, professors, engineers, and technicians, revealed themselves to be of an importance and breadth never before seen in a young party of a conspicuously social nature.[1]

In the Italian elections at the end of 1919 the popular party achieved a remarkable success. It won 100 seats in the Chamber of Deputies, and received 1,200,000 votes as against 1,500,000 for the socialists who had been organizing their supporters for over thirty years, and the party still further improved its position at the next elections in 1921. It looked like becoming the party of the future. Its failure to fulfil this early promise and to forestall the advent of fascism is a complicated story, which anyhow belongs beyond the period of this survey. In brief, it may be said that there was a right and left wing in the party, a condition which hampered firm and decisive action at critical moments. Then, the death of Benedict XV in 1922 was a severe blow to the party. His successor, Pius XI, was far from viewing it with the benevolence of his predecessor, and was conservative by disposition. His failure to encourage it was one of the factors which helped the fascists to come into power. When they did so they ruthlessly drove the popular party underground. Sturzo himself

[1] Ibid., pp. 111f.

went into exile in 1924 and did not return to Italy till 1946. In 1948 he participated in the triumph under de Gasperi's leadership of the Christian democratic party which was the popular party revived and expanded.

The aim of the present book has been to reveal how numerous and how varied were the antecedents of the Christian democrat parties and of the social catholic enterprises which, as everyone knows, have played a part of great importance in Italy and other countries since the second world war. Their emergence at that time will not seem to have been such a catholic *volte-face* as it did to many observers who were unacquainted with the history which has here been unfolded.

INDEX

Index